The Black Girl's Guide to Being Blissfully Feminine
By
Candice Adewole

This book is dedicated to my family – both blood and chosen – and all the beautiful souls who have loved me on my journey.

The Black Girl's Guide to Being Blissfully Feminine

Contents

My Journey to Being Blissfully Feminine

I did not start my life's journey being blissfully feminine. I was not one of those frou-frou girls who loved to twirl, giggle, and wear pink. I loved digging in the dirt, making mud pies, getting sweaty, and playing kickball till the street lights turned on. I hated wearing dresses, and I absolutely hated when my mother made me wear stockings. In fact, I had never even given much thought to femininity, what being feminine really was, or the importance of feminine energy until I was desperately trying to save my marriage to the man I loved.

What can I say? I was born and (mostly) raised in Cleveland, Ohio. My parents were married until I was seven years old. My dad, a Vietnam veteran, was an alcoholic and abused drugs, while my mother suffered from chronic depression. Although I have pleasant memories of them both, there was a lot of dysfunction that I remember as well. I have vivid memories of my father holding a hammer over my mother, threatening to beat her head in with it as she cried and begged him not to. I was a little girl and I remembered feeling very scared. Just recalling the memory makes me feel uncomfortable. After ten years of marriage, my mother did the right thing and left the abusive relationship in which she'd found herself.

The family I grew up with was in many ways a typical African-American family. My grandparents migrated north from Macon, Georgia to settle in Cleveland during the 1960's. They settled into a working-class neighborhood that became predominately black as all the whites moved to the suburban areas of Cleveland. By the time I was an adolescent, the neighborhood had become run down, and drugs and violence were commonplace.

Growing up in an urban environment definitely doesn't promote femininity in any way, shape, or form. Memories of my grandmother threatening, from the front porch, to beat our behinds if we didn't fight the neighborhood bully who lived next door and who was always starting trouble, or my aunt cussing out the Arabs who owned the corner store and who would, from time to time, short change us come to mind when I seek any true examples of feminine women in my early environment.

I can't honestly say that being girly, delicate, or protected was promoted to any approximation. In my neighborhood, smiling too much could make you a target for being bullied or robbed. In my family, I was ridiculed for being too sensitive.

I can honestly say that outside of the occasional hug, I don't recall any of the women in my family being what I consider affectionate. Sadly, due to some of the women in my family having negative experiences with men, the impression given was men were good for nothing, and unnecessary for happiness. Like so many women, I was raised to live life without a man.

All throughout my childhood, and up until about 10th or 11th grade, I was a tomboy. I even went through a phase of buying my clothes from the boys' department of Value City, a department store chain in Cleveland. I had bought into the feminist movement full-fledged, and started questioning why society put restrictions on women, and why women couldn't do the same things men did without the stigma. With images like the popular 90s group TLC proclaiming they weren't "too proud to beg" and 80s/90s rap icon Queen Latifah aggressively, loudly, and proudly claiming her throne, it was easy to see why I, along with other women, could so easily get caught up in the subliminal brainwashing of the time.

Despite the subconscious and conscious man-hating messages, I still ended up wanting one. Like so many young women who were abandoned by their fathers, I thought having a boyfriend and the "love" of a man would solve all the issues that were festering inside my heart. Going back over the many journals I kept as a young teen, I found that a recurring theme was needing to feel the love of a man.

I finally got a "boyfriend" at the beginning of my junior year in high school: a senior and a wannabe rapper. As with everything else that happens when you do not love yourself fully, this relationship was a disaster in the making. By the end of my senior year of high school, I was pregnant and minus a boyfriend.

It was a very depressing time because he wanted me to have an abortion, but my mother, who is very religious and with whom I lived, was against the very thought of abortion. To be honest, I wasn't sure I wanted to have one myself, so I decided to keep my baby. This caused all sorts of drama as I was bombarded by calls from my ex-boyfriend's father telling me that I had ruined his son's life and that he would make sure his son NEVER paid a dime of child support (which he did, not by choice, but that's a story for another day and time), and his mother telling me I would never be anything or do anything positive with my life now that I was to be a young mother.

I would go to my ob-gyn appointments extremely depressed. I sat there alone and looked at all the other mommies-to-be with their husbands. I had nobody to cherish the moments of hearing my daughter's heartbeat or to rub my belly at night. I would take the city bus back home from my appointments and cry. It took me years to accept that I had gotten myself into that situation, mostly because I didn't love or value myself.

Shortly after graduation, I began studying Spanish. I had developed a profound love for the Latin culture and language after going to school with Puerto Rican kids, most of whom had made their way to Cleveland after their parents left New York to find a better place for them to grow up. Listening to them speak Spanish in the hallways sparked my curiosity to understand what they were saying.

Ironically, at the same time, I began dating my first non-American man, a Puerto Rican guy born in Ponce, Puerto Rico, but raised in Miami. This man was

OBSESSED with my dark skin and thought that I was an absolute goddess because of it. He liked only dark-skinned women and had preferred them since he was young. He was a total breath of fresh air after having been made to feel unpretty by people within my community, and being rejected by men for being a dark-skinned woman.

My first encounter with different feminine cultural practices came when I attended a Puerto Rican family party. The salsa and merengue were blasting, the food was ready, and I was in a great mood. I had never had Puerto Rican food (which has heavy West African influences, by the way), so I was very excited as I made my way to the food table, helping myself to all the deliciousness to be had. I sat, and just as I was about to grab my fork to start chowing down, my boyfriend looked at me and asked where his plate was. It took me all of five seconds to scan the room and realize that all the women were getting food for their men first, so I played it off smoothly to save face and told him that I was going to get his plate, but didn't know what he wanted. I grabbed a plate, served him his food, and that was that.

I soon discovered this was a completely common and acceptable practice within Latin culture, and it became my regular habit, one I practice to this day. This was so unlike the women I grew up around, who looked down on behavior like this despite being raised with old-school southern values.

I dated Hispanic men for most of my 20's, and eventually married a Puerto Rican man. Through those relationships, I learned that, clearly, I had not been

11

groomed for married life or family life. I honestly thought that my being independent, strong, educated, articulate, and attractive made me a great catch, and that those qualities were what men looked for in a wife.

I had heard from a few men in the past that I needed to be a bit more feminine, but it didn't hit home until I was married and my ex-husband told me that I wasn't that feminine. I didn't get it; the feedback I had previously received from other men came to mind. I thought it had to do with my being a larger-framed woman, as I equated girly femininity with weight. He said no, there are big women who are feminine, but you just aren't. He couldn't fully articulate it, but something about what he said and the way he said it made me want to dig deeper. What was "being feminine"? I felt confused and my feelings were a bit hurt, too. I mean, how could I not be feminine? I wore high heels every day, my hair was styled to perfection every day, and my makeup was flawless EVERY DAY! So, if that was not feminine, I wanted to know what made a woman feminine.

Shortly after getting married, we moved to Puerto Rico. Living in Puerto Rico was a life experience I won't soon forget. So many things that could go wrong did, and it is a miracle we stayed married as long as we did.

Aside from cultural expectations being imposed on me that hadn't been prior to marriage, my ex-husband would NOT translate for me (which actually turned out to be a good thing in the end) and would verbally abuse me for the smallest things. I got called a stupid bitch more times than I care to admit, plus our car broke down. We were stuck in this little Puerto Rican town with no public transportation, and he could not find adequate work. With him being home all the time, we spent a great deal of time in each other's faces, at each other's throats, and giving each other the silent treatment. I was hurt, sad, and depressed, living away from family and friends with a husband who was being very, very difficult. Something had to change. I wanted my marriage to work.

I started listening to Jimmy Evan's Marriage Today program to figure out how I could be the woman my husband needed me to be, and the one I wanted to be. I needed to understand men in a deeper way, and thus I began my in-depth study into male psychology.

During this time, I read hundreds of books, paid for several marriage programs on male attraction, and contacted and spoke with authors of some of the books I had read. I learned so much, and all for the purpose of saving my marriage. For a period of time, our marriage did improve, but it wasn't enough.

Ultimately my ex-husband sat me down and told me he wanted a separation. After years of infrequent sex, he admitted that he no longer felt attracted to me. He told me that he didn't know exactly what had happened, but the "spark" was gone and he didn't know how to get it back. He told me he saw the changes, but he still didn't feel that sexual attraction; he felt like we were roommates.

I'll admit, I was crushed, but not terribly surprised. The issue with us not having sex had become increasingly worse and more painful. I would often approach him for sex and be turned down every time. It finally got to the point where he told me flat out not to approach him for sex because he felt like I was trying to rape him. I would cry myself to sleep every single night. I promised myself that I would never come to him for sex again.

This was very difficult for me, as I still wanted very much to have sex with him, and still felt an attraction to him. I mean, how could it be possible that he didn't want to have sex with me? After not having sex for several months of our almost 7-year relationship, he was leaving.

I looked him in the eyes and told him that although I felt very hurt and saddened to hear this, I loved him and wanted him to be happy, even if it wasn't with me. As hard as that may be to believe, it was the truth and I meant it. I didn't go off and have a crying fit or a blame session. I had learned too much about male psychology to do that. I wanted to leave a powerful impact on his psyche, and that I did.

The journey to being separated and then divorced was a difficult one. Several times he would make reappearances, claiming that he wanted to try again, but he wouldn't show up at counseling appointments. At one point, he decided he didn't want to get a divorce and refused to sign the divorce papers I had filed after a year of being separated, even though he didn't want to get back together or work on the marriage. He said he wasn't "sure." Trying to separate myself from a man I loved so dearly despite his flaws was hard.

I knew that if I was going to make it out of this emotional, category five hurricane alive, I would have to utilize the power of my femininity to come through the fire. Keeping my heart wide open, even though it hurt, was key for me.

Instead of shutting down, I let it out, I cried, and in public if I needed to. I reached out to the feminine family I had created. I cried in their arms, laughed, hugged, shared my feelings, and loved on myself.

I explored my heart, my relationships, and the deepest darkest corners of my soul to figure out why I had found myself in this relationship. What were the lessons I so desperately needed to learn so that I could love again? I was GOING to love again!

Several months after we were legally divorced, my ex-husband popped back into my life unexpectedly, saying that after dating other women, he couldn't find "another me." I wish I could say I told him to hit the road, but the truth is I had been fasting and praying for a love miracle, and this seemed like an answered prayer. I still loved him and had never fully let go of him in my spirit. He told me he wanted to date me again and give "us" another try. I was overjoyed! My family would be whole again.

We dated for 3 or 4 months, with him traveling back and forth from Virginia to visit us. It was like a dream come true; everything was going great. We soon started talking about getting back together as a couple and going to counseling. After much prayer, I realized that even though I didn't want to leave Florida, he had a great career with good pay and benefits, and because he was to be the head of the family, I needed to relocate to where he was living. At the mention of this, he was happy and told me we would discuss this further over Thanksgiving that fall.

That Thanksgiving week was amazing! He came down and we had amazing chemistry. The sexual attraction that was lost had returned, and there was plenty of kissing and sexual tension. The day after Thanksgiving we got up early to eat breakfast and take advantage of the Black Friday sales.

As we began eating, I brought up the topic of my daughter, our dogs, and I relocating to Virginia, waiting for his reply as I sipped my coffee. He looked up at me and said, "Candice, I don't think this is going to work out."

I just stared at him blankly. I absolutely could not believe what I was hearing. After almost four months of dating, he wasn't sure? I won't lie; there was a part of me that wanted to lash out at him. Instead, I told him what was on my heart and how hearing that made me feel. I also let him know that as much as I loved him, I needed to move forward with my life.

The next day, I took him to the airport and dropped him off. We said our goodbyes and I cried the entire drive home. He called me to let me know he had arrived back in Virginia safely. I never heard back from him again.

It took me about three months to fully accept he was never going to call me again. After all the fasting and praying, I didn't understand why he had been brought back into my life. I fell into a very deep depression and struggled for emotional peace. I would often sit in the shower and cry for hours. I lost my faith in God; I felt, "why bother to pray if this is the outcome?" I was determined to do two things, however, and that was to feel genuinely happy again and to love another man again. I refused to let a man who chose not to love me hold me back from truly loving myself or loving another man.

Allowing myself to be emotionally vulnerable, giving myself permission to feel all of my feelings without judgement (including the feelings of love I still had for my ex-husband), doing self-love work, and living consistently within my feminine essence, along with spiritual work and meditation, helped me find true happiness and create the heart space to fall deeply and passionately in love again.

I also noticed the principles of femininity of which I was making a habit were not only changing me, but having a powerful effect on the people around me, especially men—both men related to me and unrelated men. I was able to heal and better connect with both my father and my brothers, who were distant and uninvolved in my life.

I knew then that I needed to teach other women about the profound power of our femininity, as well as what I had learned about love and male psychology along my journey. I didn't want any other woman to suffer the way I had, and so I began working as a femininity educator and life coach to teach women how their feminine essence has the power to heal their hearts and minds, attract deeper, more intimate relationships with men, and create more peace and, overall, more satisfaction as a woman.

In the process of creating my curriculum for my class concept, I read a book called *Man Leads*. The book is based on the author's (Ro Èlori Cutno) research that she conducted to determine why Americans have such a high divorce rate in comparison to the rest of the world. After reading this manual for marriage, I felt as though it was the missing piece of the puzzle. I was so taken by the book that I reached out to the author to see if I could meet with her and discuss her book, as well as mentor with her to learn certain aspects of man charming.

After negotiating compensation for her time, I travelled to Atlanta, Georgia for about three days. There we discussed her book and she told me about a special tea ceremony she had created based on the traditional Japanese tea ceremony. She had taught a few women this tea ceremony while she was living in New Orleans. I asked her if she would teach me, and she agreed. So, after renegotiating compensation for her time to teach me the tea ceremony, I came back up to Atlanta, this time for a week, and she taught me the Japanese tea ceremony (of which I have incorporated a modified version into my Modern Day Geisha workshop).

Before I returned home, she approached me about starting a program together to educate women about femininity. Because it was in alignment with what I was already planning to do, I agreed, and together we started The Institute of Feminine Grace.

We began our Love It Up tour in Atlanta in January of 2015. It was amazingly successful, but after a few weird encounters with a few men from Facebook, we decided we would reach out to women. Our message was a well-meaning one: help African-American women, the largest group of unmarried women on planet earth, get married. What started as a co-ed retreat became Wife School.

Our first Wife School retreat was in Miami, and it was absolutely amazing. I can't say it was flawless, as cancelled flights and technical difficulties presented a challenge. However, we were able to pull it off in style, and the information given on how to be a wife was wonderful. In a matter of months, we had made stops for Wife School in several states, including California and North Carolina.

By late spring and early summer, I began to feel a bit used. As the sole financial contributor to The Institute of Feminine Grace, I realized that some of the publicity we were getting, and comments being made on social media by the author, shed a bad light on the brand, and did further damage – pushing African-American women further away rather than drawing them in. This was very disconcerting to me.

Granted, I had agreed to be the sole financial contributor, because the author had her book and she told me that she had a possible deal on the table with the Cosby family, as well as other projects that she could be busy with instead, and that she had a large following on Facebook, so I should consider my contribution an investment in my own future. Perhaps I was a bit naïve…okay, maybe a lot…but I agreed. I soon saw the social media blunders as major fails, including the author's use of Liris's (the famous plus-sized model) image for a tee shirt campaign, which turned into a horrible social media storm that went viral on both Twitter and Facebook when the author refused to take down the photo in the time frame that Liris gave. Even after I discussed my concerns and urged her to remove the photo, she seemed unbothered and assured me this sandstorm would pass, and that the publicity was good, even though we ended up getting our Facebook pages temporarily shut down due to Liris's fans reporting us.

We also took another huge hit when she decided to address slain activist Sandra Bland's death by creating a meme that said "Let's face it, if Sandra Bland had a husband, she would still be alive." When she posted it privately asking for thoughts, I told her that I did not think the meme was a good idea, that it was not going to be well-received, and the point she was trying to make about the importance of black women having the protection of a husband would be lost, not to mention that the timing was insensitive to the many people hurting because of this young woman's untimely passing. I was told she was not asking for my permission, but letting me know in advance that she was going to post this meme. I immediately contacted the website designer and asked to have my personal contact information removed because I was scared and anticipated the drama this would cause.

I was very wise in doing this, because all the drama ended up making headlines on Huffington Post. Hate mail flooded our inbox, as did death threats, which were extremely unsettling.

Emotionally, I was in turmoil for a variety of reasons. I cared about the well-being of Ro, the relationships I had built with all the ladies from the Wife School retreats, and the Facebook group, but by late fall, several things were taking their toll: the negativity, certain passive aggressive behaviors, being periodically accused of jealousy (any time I addressed her negative and passive aggressive behaviors), at the fact that she had gotten married before I did and was having a baby with her now-husband after a short courtship. I was starting to feel as though I was in the female version of my marriage with my ex-husband.

There were moments when I would communicate my feelings, apologize when it was really I who deserved an apology, and suck it up to maintain the personal and professional relationship I had developed, but I came to the conclusion after over a year that some people are who they are; they do not see anything wrong with their behavior and will most likely never change. Thus, they have to be removed from your life, which is precisely what I did.

It was difficult and I felt like I was going through a real breakup. It was a hard decision to make on so many levels because I really wanted The Institute of Feminine Grace, in which I had invested close to $30,000 of my own money, to succeed in restoring the feminine spirit of African-American women and the integrity of the black family.

I tried to handle my departure gracefully, but, sadly, came under attack on social media. Ro, a former mutual friend, and several of her devotees slandered my name and spied on me. This made me feel so horribly sad. My heart hurt so badly.

I was ready to completely give up on educating women about the beauty of living in their feminine essence until I caught word that a sweet young woman I knew had gotten banned from and thrown out of The Institute of Feminine Grace for questioning and disagreeing with Ro. I was saddened because I knew this young woman was such a beautiful spirit and needed sisterhood, not chastisement.

I knew then that someone from the African-American community needed to stand up for, and teach, authentic femininity and feminine grace, and Blissfully Feminine was born. Blissfully Feminine would focus on teaching women authentic femininity and healthy masculinity, because if a woman isn't authentically feminine, she won't be able to attract and keep a good, healthy man or be genuinely happy and fulfilled in her life as a woman.

My journey has served as a testimony to how being Blissfully Feminine can free your heart to experience the best of life and make it through the tough times. I look back at all of my life experiences with joy now because I have learned so much, without which I wouldn't be the woman I am today.

It is my greatest desire that you utilize this guide to enhance your life and glean what good you can to empower yourself, heal your heart, and experience the best in every area of life. I want you to win, sister! I want you to love yourself; I want you to fall madly in love with a good man who will love, and take care of, and protect you. I want your families to have generational excellence, and I want you to enjoy your life being Blissfully Feminine!

1. Feminine Mystique

"Pretty women wonder where my secret lies.
I'm not cute or built to suit a fashion model's size
But when I start to tell them,
They think I'm telling lies.
I say,
It's in the reach of my arms
The span of my hips,
The stride of my step,
The curl of my lips.
I'm a woman
Phenomenally.
Phenomenal woman,
That's me."
- *Maya Angelou*

In a society that promotes letting it all hang out, we as a culture are obsessed with reality TV, Instagram, Snapchatting, Periscoping, and the like. We want to know what's going on in the lives of others. Sharing the details of what we do and how we do it has become a sort of national pastime.

Very little is sacred and very little is secret. A woman who has a bit of mystery is a rare breed. The woman who knows what to reveal and how much to reveal is a rare jewel, indeed.

When I think of the feminine mystique, I think of the courtesans of old, or the Japanese Geisha: women who allured many and aroused curiosity simply because they were mysterious.

Sadly, somewhere between the Real World and the Real Housewives of Atlanta, women have lost their feminine mystique. From wearing scanty outfits that barley cover one's nudity to twerking on YouTube, the modern-day American woman leaves very little to the imagination. The interesting thing is that with respect to the arts of seduction and male attraction, men are more attracted to and love a woman who is a bit more mysterious. You see, men love the thrill of the hunt, the allure of the unknown, and this is why a man will always be more drawn to a woman who presents a chase through the power of her feminine mystique. Aside from this fact, women who have feminine mystique are perceived as being classier and wiser.

A woman who has lost her feminine mystique also risks diminishing the sexual attraction her man has for her. It is important for a woman to become consciously aware of maintaining her feminine mystique.

Here are a few ways you can maintain your feminine mystique.

1.) Keep what number you have to do in the bathroom to yourself. Nobody needs to know you have to pee really badly. Also, do not use the bathroom in front of your man, I don't care how comfortable you all are with each other.

2.) Keep your beauty routine to yourself. I mean, we are thankful for all the YouTube contouring videos on how to get your face beat and brows perfectly arched, but now all the guys know how we get pretty. Keep a few beauty secrets to yourself.

3.) Speaking of, avoid getting dressed and pretty in front of your man.

4.) Don't reveal how many sexual partners you've had (DO reveal if you have STD's/STI's, or children). Revealing to a man the number of sex partners you've had will likely decrease your chances of marriage to him, as men use that number to determine whether or not you are wife-able (I know, it's not fair, but it's masculine instinct). For most men, anything over 2 or 3 is A LOT. Just don't disclose that number. This also goes for any freaky-deaky sexual rendezvous you've had as well.

5.) When getting to know people, especially men, gradually divulge details about yourself. People shouldn't know your entire life story within one hour of meeting you.

2. The Power of Touch

"When I touched her body,
I believed she was God.
In the curves of her form
I found the birth of Man,
the creation of the world,
and the origin of all life."
— **Roman Payne**

The one thing I learned from living in Puerto Rico in a Latin-American culture is they LOVE to touch one another. In Latin culture, you kiss on the cheek upon greeting. Women (and men) are very physically affectionate with everyone, and hugs are given freely without any reservations.

I noticed this same thing on my travels to Paris, France. Women (and men) were very affectionate and attentive. Most of the couples I saw there were holding hands or walking arm in arm.

Because I spent half of my life in African-American culture and the other half of my life in Latin culture, I can see the stark differences in the levels of affection and attention women give across the board. Within the African-American community (the only exception would be southern women, but even then the levels of physical affection are not that of Latin cultures), we don't give a great deal of physical affection in general.

Several years ago when I finally went back to visit my hometown of Cleveland after living in Miami for a few years, I realized that I longed for two things: speaking and hearing Spanish, and kisses and touching! I didn't even realize there was such a lack of affection in our culture until I had immersed myself in another culture and gone home for a visit.

There is an interesting science behind touch. "Touch is the first of the senses to develop in the human infant, and it remains perhaps the most emotionally central throughout our lives." (thenewyorker.com)

"…among humans, touch might seem to serve as little more than a proxy for social bonds. If we often experience friendly or loving caresses, it's safe to assume that we have a strong social network, which is itself one of the best predictors of happiness, health, and longevity." (newyorker.com)

So it is safe to say that people who touch each other frequently are happier and healthier, and live longer. People who touch frequently also have stronger social bonds and ties to others in their communities.

"According to Dr. Fran Walfish, celebrity doctor and author, cuddling is healthy for people because of the obvious factor of emotional attachment." … "Oxytocin is a neuropeptide that is closely linked to childbirth and breastfeeding, and a recent study shows that it has a biological role in bonding between mother and baby." (www.shape.com) Oxytocin is also released whenever we hug each other.

Besides bonding and happiness, hugging and kissing can reduce the risk of heart disease by the secretion of oxytocin, and can reduce stress levels and anxiety. Communication between partners is increased when there is a lot of physical affection.

My beloved sisters, this is one area I feel we need to consciously make an effort to improve in. Touching is a form of nurturing, and as feminine women, that is what we do: nurture.

In my family, on both sides, there is not much physical affection in general. Hugs upon greeting, but definitely no kissing. Also, I never witnessed much physical affection among others in my community outside of hugging upon greeting.

Men need touch to fully receive appreciation. I know that may sound strange, but it's true. Men actually NEED touch accompanied by verbal praise or appreciation to fully receive the appreciation (it's a subconscious, psychological thing). Men are hardwired to PROTECT, PROVIDE, and PROCREATE. They want to make us happy, and because of their desire to please us, they live for validation in the form of appreciation.

This touch can be in the form of a pat on the back, a gentle touch on the hand while saying thank you, or even a blow job (for your husband or fiancé) if your man has done something extraordinarily awesome for you. Also, lots of physical affection like French kissing, holding hands, or a pat on the butt lets others know that you and your man are connected and together!

I know that some of you may need to work gradually on being more physically affectionate, and if you are a survivor of sexual, verbal, or physical abuse, or have witnessed this type of abuse growing up, this may feel a bit challenging, but it must be done.

I am a survivor of sexual and verbal abuse. I was always an affectionate child, but I remember my abuser telling me to stop being all touchy-feely because somebody might think "something was going on." That comment always struck me as odd, and always stayed in the back of my mind. Even to this day, I remember that comment and exactly where we were when it was said to me. I was seven years old. As a result, I remember feeling weird about giving hugs and being touched.

Living within Latin American culture really helped heal that part of me because I was able to witness first hand that touching was NORMAL; it was fun, bonding, and a healthy part of relationships between family members and friends, no matter how casually or intimately you knew the person.

As a part of my work as a femininity educator, I am ALWAYS interviewing men, talking to them, and getting inside their brains to help women like you understand them better. One of the most repeated comments made by American men who travel overseas is about the stark contrast in the levels of affection given by women in other countries and that of American women. African-American men who travel to places like Brazil and the Dominican Republic almost ALWAYS say the one thing they love the most is the feminine nurturing in the form of touch. I know firsthand EXACTLY what they are talking about.

Now, I know that you may be rolling your eyes at me at this point, but I encourage you to keep an open mind and heart because I am coming from a place of love and because there is ALWAYS room for improvement.

Also, we need to make sure that we are physically affectionate with our children, both boys and girls, hugging, holding, and kissing them frequently, and encouraging them to be affectionate with their siblings (if any) to keep them feeling loved and bonded to you and one another. Touching your children frequently is important to their emotional development as well as their overall wellbeing. Far too often I have heard, "Put that baby down or you're going to spoil him/her." This couldn't be further from the truth, and I think that the notion of it is a bit dysfunctional.

I advise touching and holding your babies, even grown children, frequently. I still allow my daughter, who is in her late teens, to curl up on me while I hug and rub her. This should never stop, in my opinion.

Below is a list of ways you can incorporate touch to make it a natural part of your practice as a feminine woman. Touch is infectious and, once it is practiced, you will find that people open up to you more. Our nurturing touch is one of our super powers as women. This is part of feminine nurturing and you can't effectively nurture anyone to excellence without touching them.

1. Make kissing and hugging family members upon entering and leaving the house a part of your family's practice.

2. Greet people with hugs instead of a handshake or a hug only after shaking their hand. This will catch some people off guard in our Western culture, but it is almost always appreciated. Trust me when I say that most Americans are STARVING for a hug. Quick side story: My daughter, who is autistic, had to be taken to urgent care a few months ago. She is ALWAYS hugging everyone, so before leaving, she hugged the nurse practitioner as we were walking out the door. The nurse looked at my daughter and said, "Wow, thank you. I haven't been hugged in years." I thought, *how sad*. Sadly, she is not alone. As a society, Americans don't touch enough, and are too worried about "personal space." So, yes, please DO hug others!

3. Kiss friends and family on the cheek. It's okay to steal other POSITIVE cultural practices and make them your own. I absolutely LOVE the Latin cultural practice of kissing on the cheeks when greeting and leaving. In Spanish-speaking countries, it's one kiss on the right cheek, while in Brazil and France it's two kisses, first the right cheek (the person's right, your left), then the left cheek.

4. Pat the back. There's something affirming and accepting about a good pat on the back.

5. Touch arms, face, and legs when talking to your man. Done in the right places and at the right time, it will draw him into you more!

By incorporating more touch and affection with the Black Girl Magic we already have, girl, we will STAY winning! Black Girl Magic is some of the most powerful magic on earth, so go ahead, reach out and touch your neighbor!

3. Travel

"Why do women want to dress like men when they're fortunate enough to be women? Why lose femininity, which is one of our greatest charms? We get more accomplished by being charming than we would be flaunting around in pants and smoking. I'm very fond of men. I think they are wonderful creatures. I love them dearly. But I don't want to look like one. When women gave up their long skirts, they made a grave error…"
— **Tasha Tudor**

Get yourself a passport, my love. Whatever you do this year, make it your priority, and if you are married and/or have children, get passports for your husband and kids.

Contrary to popular belief, international travel isn't that expensive. There are all sorts of cool, creative, and inexpensive ways to travel internationally these days. Depending on the time of year, it's actually cheaper to fly to Paris, France from the East Coast than to fly to Los Angeles!

The reason I've included travel in the *Black Girl's Guide to Being Blissfully Feminine* is because I believe that African-American people, in particular women, suffer from low self-esteem and depression, more than any other group of people, due to not having a strong cultural foundation, and living within a society built on racism, color, and class. Travel can help with this problem.

International travel will help you realize there are many, many places on the planet where being a brown woman isn't that big of a deal (by the way, brown and black people are the majority on the planet), or actually a benefit to you. Going to places where people are fascinated by your brown skin is a self-esteem booster like you wouldn't believe! Having men chase you in the streets to tell you they are completely fascinated with your rich, dark skin and that you are unlike any other woman they have ever seen is an amazing experience that I wish for every black girl to have. I'm telling you, the Black Girl Magic is REAL!

Seeing other black people throughout the African diaspora will also help you feel part of a larger, global black community. When you realize there are more black people living in Brazil than in the United States (actually, there are more black people in all of South America than in the United States and the Caribbean), and that they have retained much of the African culture, it will give you a sense of pride to be part of a global African community. Personally, I have had a more authentic African experience by participating in Afro-Latin culture, by intermingling with Afro-Cubans and Puerto Ricans, and by learning the African influenced dances, drum rhythms, and religions. Through them, I have been able to reconnect with what I've missed out on in African-American culture.

Travel is truly a healing experience for the black girl's soul. It will open your heart and mind for the better.

This past summer, in France, I had a wonderful experience. People were very eager to learn more about me because I was African-American. The number-one question I was asked was why police officers kill unarmed black people. Which was shocking to me. They couldn't understand it (since this type of thing doesn't happen over there), and were absolutely alarmed and disgusted that no arrests have ever been made despite it being on video (this was the reaction from everyone who asked me, including "white" Frenchman). They also loved telling me they loved President Obama and First Lady Michelle Obama because they were "black." It was so funny to me — and cute!

Travel will also open your eyes to how masculine American women have become across the board. It is very interesting to observe how women from different cultures behave and interact with men. In my experience, these feminine cultural takeaways have only added to my feminine nature.

At this point you may be wondering how you can begin your world tour. I've gathered a few helpful tips so that you can travel inexpensively!

1. House Swap – This is a really cool idea I got from VergeMagazine.com. Essentially, you pick a location you want to travel to and find people from that country who would be willing to swap houses with you. Of course, you have to be careful and screen potential swappers. There are a few websites that advertise this type of arrangement. (I

even have a friend who did it to go to Cabos San Lucas, Mexico for the cost of airfare and food.) Homeexchange.com and Homeexchangevacation.com are two sites to try!

2. Budget Airfare – I belong to a travel discount club called Surge365. However, there are always great travel deals online. You can also look at budget airlines like flymonarch.com or jetstar.com.

3. Become an international au pair for families that want an English-speaking nanny for their kids. I think this is an AWESOME idea for single women and single moms. If you love working with children, this is an option for you. You get to live in another country with room and board, paid expenses, and a paycheck while being able to absorb the culture and language! There are a few websites dedicated to this, but I'll list the most popular one: www.aupaircare.com/childcare

4. Travel during the low/off season. This is a great option for a variety of reasons. Low costs, plus not as crowded!

5. Try hostels instead of pricey hotels. You'd be surprised at some of the decent hostel options out there. Airbnb is also a great alternative to pricey hotels; I have used Airbnb quite a bit in my travels. I also recommend using Innclusive.com. Relatively new on the market, it is an AirBnB-like service, created by an African-American gentleman after having a few negative experiences using Airbnb.

4. Know Your Roots

I was born in the congo
I walked to the fertile crescent and built
the sphinx
I designed a pyramid so tough that a star
that only glows every one hundred years falls
into the center giving divine perfect light
I am bad
-Nikki Giovanni

Somewhere between Queen Nefertiti and Nicki Minaj we got confused. Somewhere between the greatness of the upper Nile Valley and the middle passage we lost our way, our ancestral knowledge, our femininity, our softness. We forgot who we were and who we are.

It is so very important to know your roots, your history, and where your people come from. This knowledge is one of the key pieces that make up the foundation of your self-esteem. Of all black women, African-American women are probably the most proud to be of African descent, but they know so little about their African heritage and traditions.

I am very blessed to have an Alex Haley, *Roots*-type story in my family. The story of our family coming as enslaved Africans around the early 1600s, and being from

Nigeria and present-day Ghana, of the Mandinka, Yoruba, and Songhai tribes, has been passed down from generation to generation. There are also a few stories from the enslavement period of one of my ancestors going to rescue his daughter and wife from a neighboring plantation where they'd been sold, and who ran off to live with the Native Americans.

A few summers ago, our family did an AfricanAncestry.com DNA test, which confirmed that we are 80% West African, from Nigeria and Ghana! How cool is that? We also did an AfricanAncestry.com DNA test on my maternal side and discovered that we descend from the Balanta people of West Africa.

Having this knowledge is monumental for me; I am not an orphan child with unknown origins. I have a history, a story, a people, traditions…AND SO DO YOU!

As a people, we often get stuck on the 400-year enslavement period and the reconstruction period that followed (our people are still in a period of reconstruction). We are so stuck that we forget that our people enjoyed over 10,000 years of HIGH CIVILIZATION!

We come from greatness; we come from order, immense creativity, and structure. Our roots are based in traditional family values.

Many times we focus on the warrior queens of Africa, but we forget about our tradition of femininity and the variety of traditions that supported the energy balance between men and women. We forget we had a soft, gentle side as African women.

I lovingly encourage you to look beyond the plantation of the south, to go past the middle passage and rediscover the greatness of your African roots. Your femininity and self-esteem depend on it.

There are many ways you can – and I believe should – embrace your African roots. One beautiful way is to take some form of African dance regularly. Feminine movement is beautiful and keeps you feeling sensual and juicy. That coupled with cultural rhythms will keep you grounded, mind, body, and spirit.

1)Incorporate African drumming at family events and gatherings. Have your sons learn African drumming and buy a drum for your house. Our people NEED to hear the drums again. Drums need to be a regular part of our lives and social events. The drums have ALWAYS been the heartbeat of our African people. Sadly, African-Americans are the only group within the African diaspora that has lost the drumming as a regular part of life. From my travels, I have found African drumming to be a normal part of life in Puerto Rico, in Cuba, in Brazil, in Guadalupe, and every other place where Africans landed. So I implore you to go back and get it, SANKOFA! There is NO SHAME in returning to retrieve that which was lost.

2)I also suggest at important family gatherings such as weddings, baby showers, funerals, family reunions, graduation parties, and other such celebrations, that you encourage everyone to wear African attire. This is done in Africa to this day, and it is simply beautiful to adorn yourself in traditional ways. We wear western style clothes most of the time, so it makes family gatherings even that much more special when you include this piece of culture.

3)Another excellent way to reconnect to your African roots is by starting a rites-of-passage ceremony in your family, place of worship, or community. There are many beautiful rites-of-passage traditions for women in the diverse African cultures. We actually implemented one called Duafe a few years back, and it was so wonderful and emotional because we knew that it was our responsibility to teach our daughters their culture and the ways of womanhood.

4)Finally, I highly recommend you get a DNA test done. There are many out there, but I like AfricanAncestry.com. They specifically deal with African ancestry, and you get a certificate saying what tribe you come from. They can also give you a breakdown of any other races/ethnic groups found in your DNA.

You have no idea the tremendous amount of self-confidence, joy, and healing you will get from knowing EXACTLY where you come from. You will also find closure because no longer will you be a lost child without an ancestral homeland.

5. What to Do with Your Mouth

"Those of us who embrace the feminine know its strength."
— <u>Betsy Cornwell</u>

Growing up, my mother would say, "Candice, if I see you being loud or talking with your mouth stretched open so wide I can see all down your throat, I'ma pop you." My mother absolutely detested seeing other black women being unnecessarily loud and ignorant in public. Being loud at family parties, yes. In public? Um, NO!

I know this will be a sensitive topic for many (but please hear me out), because as black women we pride ourselves on how well we verbally let people know what we are feeling. With necks rolling and fingers waving, black women are particularly skilled at putting together the just the right combination of words to let a person know precisely what is on their minds, be it good or bad.

Our mouths. The power of life and death are in the tongue, says Proverbs 18:21. Many say this, but I don't know how many actually believe this.

As women, we have so much power with our words and the sounds of our voices. Our words and voices are two of the ways we can nurture those around us. Men use the tone and inflection of our voices to gauge whether we are pleased, whether we can be pleased, or whether they want to bother trying to please us at all. We can build up or tear down with our words.

Let's start with the actual sound of our voices. Many black women (in general) have raspier, deeper voices than other women do. Our voices aren't very high pitched or nasally, and because of this we can sometimes come off as harsh or abrasive even if we don't mean to.

I believe that every woman has a girly, feminine voice. This is the soft voice we use when talking to babies and animals, or when talking over the phone to that guy who makes our hearts race. This voice is the voice we should use most of the time.

In your home, your voice shouldn't be the predominate one in the house. Yelling across the house to get someone's attention is convenient, but VERY unladylike. To maintain the feminine energy balance in your home, your voice should be only a few notches higher than a whisper. If you need to get someone's attention in your house, you either need to actually get up and go to them if they can't hear you, or, if you are feeling extra lazy, text them. Being too loud is obnoxious, harsh, overbearing, masculine, and rude. Our aim is to polish our femininity. Our voices as women should be soothing, relaxing, and nurturing, and add to the overall peace of any environment in which we find ourselves.

Let's explore how our voices affect the men in our lives. There is much to be said about how our voices affect men. Our voices can either serenade him, or irritate him and turn him off. This leads me to discuss how we navigate disagreements with our man verbally without disrespecting him and turning him off.

In relationships, there will always be situations that make us feel angry, disappointed, or sad. The key to navigating these moments is to stay in the feminine zone. You may naturally start yelling or talking loud when you get mad or irritated with your man, but please understand this: When you yell, scream, or loud talk your man, it is his masculine instinct to respond to you as though you are another man. He will likely raise his voice to compete for space and show his dominance (masculine instinct). A man wants to naturally be the lead in his space, his territory. When you start getting manly with your man, you will trigger his instinct to secure his territory. You are no longer an MVP at this point, you are an opponent.

However, we can use our voices to our advantage to not only calm the situation, but to negotiate and get what we want. This is FEMININE POWER!

When you and your man are having a disagreement and you feel yourself reaching high levels of anger and frustration, you must say in a low voice, "Baby, I understand that we are both upset, but I *really want to respect you*. I really need your help to work this out, and I want us to both be heard." Then stay silent and wait for his help. You should also incorporate feminine touch and feminine body posture so that he can visually take in that you are respecting him. This may take some practice, especially if you are used to verbally emasculating your man by saying whatever you want, however you want. This may also shock your man if he is used to you flying off the handle. You will need to inform him that you are learning and growing as a woman, and that this is your new practice to bring peace and respect to him, your relationship, and the family. Being that men NEED very HIGH levels of respect to fully receive love, if he is emotionally healthy, he will be open to your new method of communicating.

Men are hardwired to problem solve, so this method of communicating verbally will both give him respect and trigger his desire to help you. As long as you keep your voice soft and feminine, even while upset, your man will be triggered to protect and comfort you, not go into toe-to-toe combat with you.

There are other times when you may need to keep your mouth closed and not talk at all, especially as it relates to men. Men are much more visual and action oriented than women are, whereas women are much more verbal than men are. Men understand actions, while women relate to words.

I have learned from many mentors, and I learned a very valuable relationship tool from the last mentor I worked with, which I will share with you. This tool is a real jewel and can even help in the most difficult situations. This technique is called Feminine Silence.

Feminine Silence is a technique in which you do absolutely NO TALKING. Depending on the severity of the issue, you may need to go into Feminine Silence for a few hours, or a month or two (YES, I'm serious). Here's the key, though, that differentiates Feminine Silence from the passive-aggressive silent treatment: You are still being

NICE and LOVING during the period of silence. You are still cooking, serving food, being nurturing, smiling, etc. Also during this time, you are processing your emotions, examining yourself, journaling, meditating, praying, reflecting, and crying if need be.

Men know that women LOVE to talk, so by not talking, you will capture his attention. Best believe a woman who is NOT talking AND still being nice is going to spark his curiosity. He is going to ask "Is anything wrong?" This is when you will tell him in a soft voice that you need his help with what's going on, and that you aren't feeling assertive. He will be willing to work through the issues. This is your chance to be open and vulnerable and use your feminine communication skills (which I go deeper into in my Domestic Goddess Society Programs). Connecting to his heart and triggering his masculine instinct to problem solve, protect you, and be vulnerable too is how you use your feminine energy to bridge the relationship.

6. A Word About Bad Words & Cursing

Today, saying bad words has become commonplace. The lines of social etiquette have become blurred as women have strived to prove they don't need anybody telling them what they should or shouldn't do, including what they shouldn't do with their mouths. I've seen some women drop more F-bombs in one sentence than were dropped on D-day.

As a rule of thumb, the feminine woman shouldn't curse/say bad words in public or in front of children. It's just poor etiquette and signifies an ill upbringing. Personally, I don't like saying bad words (although admittedly I do from time to time, but I am working to stop this because words embody spirits and bad words carry loads of negative energy). With all that being said, if you must express yourself with expletives, do it in private and avoid cursing in front of men at all costs (or in private, just the two of you, and even then keep it at a minimum). Why? Because, dear sweet sister, we must preserve our sweet, feminine, delicate nature. Cursing is viewed as harsh, abrasive, masculine, and manly, and doing so makes you look and sound masculine. Masculine women appear strong, and strong women don't need masculine protection. We want the opposite effect. We want to be viewed as soft, feminine women who need masculine protection and who are worthy of protecting.

A final word on bad words. For mothers out there who love to tell their kids, "I'm gonna whoop your a$$," or who cuss out their kids sideways, I urge you to stop and reconsider. This is not effective parenting; it is residual slave-mentality behavior that has likely been passed down in your family and that doesn't lead to generational excellence. We must use our mouths to nurture and build up our children.

7. Names of Affection

I am so perfect so divine so ethereal so surreal
I cannot be comprehended
except by my permission
-Nikki Giovanni

Which leads me to affectionate pet names. Using pet names is extremely important. Many women in this day and age do not use pet names on a regular basis, nor do they see the importance of it.

Men absolutely LOVE when their women use pet names, especially in front of others, provided that the pet name isn't emasculating. Our children also need us to use frequent pet names so that they feel special and nurtured. Many American women feel uncomfortable doing this, but it must become our regular practice.

Using pet names, especially during tense moments, can ease the air and create a way to smooth things over. I love using pet names, and I do it with everyone. I became more open to this by observing Hispanic women, who I think win hands down when it comes to using pet names. They are unapologetic about it, and it's a cultural nugget we can learn from. They love using Papi, mi amor (my love), mi vida (my life), or linda or lindo (pretty one, or cute).

If you are not used to using pet names all the time, it will feel weird and a bit silly at first, but like anything, with practice it will become normal. Reserve creative and exclusive pet names you don't use with anyone else for your loved ones!

Here is a list of cute pet names you can start incorporating right away!

Papi
Cherie
Angel Eyes
Super Hero
Amazing
Big Papa
Boo
Boo Thang
Superman
Bull
Captain
Chief
Cowboy
Daddy
Handsome
Good Lookin'
Hero
Hershey Kiss
My King
Soldier

8. Take Off Your Cape

"Think like a queen. A queen is not afraid to fail. Failure is another steppingstone to greatness." – Oprah Winfrey

Superwoman: That's who we have been for far too long, and often without a Superman to help us.

We do everything for everyone. We are everything for everyone. We are mother, grandmother, lover, friend, teacher, healer, worker, driver, prayer warrior, enforcer, cook, and more, rolled into one.

Somehow we have managed to do it. Somehow we have learned to embrace this Superwoman role. Somehow we think this is normal, the way things are supposed to be. We are "strong" black women, we can do anything and everything…or can we?

You want to know what I think? I think the cape we wear and the "S" on our chests is just a cover up. Underneath the Superwoman outfit is a woman who is vulnerable, soft, and loving. A woman who wants Superman to take the load off so she doesn't have to do everything by herself. So that she can be girly, and fun, and playful. So that she can be all the things all the women before her couldn't be.

When I think of the strong black Superwoman, I can't help but think of that scene from *Gone With the Wind*, in which actress Hattie McDaniel's character is helping the character Scarlett O'Hara get dressed. There is something about that image that just hits the very core of me as a woman. Here is a woman who had to sit on the sidelines while other women got to be soft, pretty, and loved. All she got to be was overworked and ignored. How sad!

The images of black women on display in the mass media, from music videos to the silver screen, are still overwhelmingly masculine and oversexualized. Kerri Washington's character, Olivia Pope, on the popular T.V. show "Scandal" comes to mind. Here you have an intelligent, formally educated, accomplished African-American woman who is beautiful, poised, and well put together, yet she is hard and emotionally unavailable. Her energy is overwhelmingly masculine, not to mention the fact that she's single and having an affair (at least the last time I watched) with the President of the United States.

Or take "The Real Housewives of Atlanta". All the women are gorgeous, successful (in masculine terms of success), and intelligent, yet masculine in their energy, bossy, and at times rude and mean. Or you have the super ratchet types as seen on "The Maury Povich Show" that are masculine, mean, loud, and classless.

These images further perpetuate the general consensus that we are strong, loud, abrasive, in your face, hard, and sexual. A woman like this doesn't need protection or provision because she's got everything under control. A woman like this definitely doesn't trigger the masculine instinct in a man to want to marry her and take care of her.

I can read your mind at this point: "But we ARE strong." I understand that as a group of women we have withstood a great deal of abuses and injustices, and it is a miracle that we are still here making the strides we have, but still, Superwoman must take off her cape.

African-American women have the highest rates of breast cancer, cervical cancer, high blood pressure, mental health problems, and obesity (which leads to many health issues), and we have the highest rate of smokers among "minority" groups in this country. I truly think most of this is due to us being pushed to be masculine, being overworked, and trying to do and be everything for everyone.

It's time to retire your cape. You have the opportunity for the first time in many generations to reclaim the power of your femininity. To be soft, to be girly, to be playful, and to live an awesomely happy life and enjoy being a woman.

Ways You Can Retire the Cape

1) Cut Off Negative People – Negative people will drain you, use you, and suck you dry. If you keep them around, they will leave you with very little energy to polish your femininity, or they will so drain you emotionally that you will be in masculine energy too much.

2) Avoid Other People's Problems – Do not unnecessarily involve yourself in other people's problems. You don't have to save everybody, and

this includes your siblings AND grown children. Learn to create boundaries for yourself.

3) Ask For Help – Many are afraid to ask for help due to a fear of being rejected. Admitting that you need help and then asking for it – and being OPEN to receive the help – keeps you very feminine. You can ask just about anyone for help. I personally have recruited my neighbor's sons to be my grocery bag helpers. They love helping Miss Candice take all her grocery bags into the house, and I love it, too! One less thing I have to do alone. I have also recruited an older neighbor to be my lawn husband. He does my lawn care whenever he does his. I give him plenty of appreciation and some home-cooked food once in a while. A total WIN/WIN! Asking for help requires trust and vulnerability. This may feel uncomfortable, but it's necessary for you to get into feminine energy.

4) Avoid Doing As Many Masculine Tasks As Possible – This includes taking out the garbage, mowing the lawn, and fixing your car.

5) Create Community – Build a community of other women who are positive, feminine, and trustworthy. Gather a list of the group's talents, then come together to help one another. Be there for one another when needed. Babysit or cook food when someone is sick. Feminine women create and bridge communities!

I thoroughly detest being called a "strong" black woman for its masculine connotation, the underlying implication that I am somehow built for hard labor, like some animal, and that I am undeserving to be treated like a lady who needs (and wants) to be protected, cared for, adored, cherished, and treated gently.

I prefer to be called a feminine black woman or a resilient black woman because, although technically a synonym of the word "strong," the meaning feels better and more feminine. Resilience and personal fortitude are what you must have mentally and emotionally to get through tough times. I don't want to be "strong." I DO need a man, I DO want help, I DO want to be taken care of and protected. I DO need community, and I wear dresses, not capes. I'm not a pushover, I'm not Superwoman. I am a resilient woman, I have dropped my cape, and I cordially invite you to drop yours, too.

9. Smile & Laugh

Femininity is not just lipstick, stylish hairdos, and trendy clothes. It is the divine adornment of humanity. It finds expression in your qualities of your capacity to love, your spirituality, delicacy, radiance, sensitivity, creativity, charm, graciousness, gentleness, dignity, and quiet strength. - James E. Faust

We have all walked into the store and seen that one cashier with the stank attitude face, who just refuses to crack a smile at all, or we have walked into a room in which all the women look us up and down. Many times I personally want to say, "It's going to be okay, it's not going to kill you if you smile!"

Stank face is a serious problem in our community of women, as is the lesser offense, RBF (Resting Bitch Face) as people call it these days. I think that there are a number of reasons why some women wear a permanent scowl on their faces, including feelings of having to be Superwoman, growing up in harsh urban environments, and just not being aware of their facial gestures.

Smile, my beautiful sisters, smile! Smiling is probably one of the easiest things you can do to show that you have positive energy. Smiling is also the universal sign of happiness, contentment, and peace. Not to mention, you just look prettier when you smile.

Let's face it, black women are winning in the beauty department. We have very sought-after features, especially our lips and butts. Everyone wants full, thick lips, and we have been genetically blessed with them naturally! This, in and of itself, is a HUGE reason to smile.

A woman who smiles a lot is also generally seen as approachable and easy to please. Men are absolutely smitten and drawn to women who smile because it signifies she is happy, confident, nurturing, and easy to please. It is also a signal there is a low chance of him being rejected, so women who smile get approached by men more often.

If you feel like you don't have a pretty smile, get in front of the mirror and practice smiling until it feels natural (this is what I had to do when I was younger). As you are growing in your femininity, make it your practice to smile wherever you go.

Some FUN facts about smiling:

1. Forcing yourself to smile can boost your mood.
2. Smiling boosts your immune system.
3. Smiles are contagious and so is laughter.
4. Smiles relieve stress.
5. It is easier to smile than to frown.

If you still struggle with finding reasons to smile and laugh, I recommend keeping a gratitude journal. If you understand anything about Universal Law, you will know that love and gratitude (giving thanks) are the two highest vibrational energies in the universe.

When I was recovering from my emotional breakdown a few years ago, keeping a gratitude journal revitalized my hope that things could and would get better. In the beginning it felt a bit ridiculous to give thanks for finding delicious gluten-free bread and for having nice teeth, but each day I found something new to add to the list, and that alone made me smile.

You have the right to be happy and smile! You have the right to be open, girly, carefree, and full of laughs. So go ahead and give yourself permission to BE HAPPY & SMILE!

10. Emotional Vulnerability

Don't be afraid to feel as angry or as loving as you can, because when you feel nothing, it's just death.
-Lena Horne

In my years of serving as a femininity educator and life coach, I found that being emotionally vulnerable is probably one of the toughest hurdles for women to get over. The thought of opening one's heart for all to see, the thought of sharing your true, authentic feelings, your mind, and your soul can be very scary for some.

Often, due to being abused as a child, or growing up with emotionally damaged people, or not being brought up with the proper love and support, we learn to be emotionally closed or unavailable as a defense mechanism. Getting hurt feels bad, so we make internal vows that we won't let anyone or anything hurt us ever again. Or if we have been in and out of several unsuccessful, emotionally draining relationships, or abusive relationships, we will make that decision to keep our hearts closed.

However, when we keep our hearts closed from getting hurt, we also keep love from getting in. You simply cannot experience high levels of deep love with a closed heart.

In order to heal, we must abandon the notion that men are bad, or that love hurts, or any of the other false beliefs we have. We must make being emotionally vulnerable a top priority. We must make being loved fully a top priority.

To become emotionally vulnerable, one must be aware of their feelings and learn how to properly express them in a feminine way. In both my Modern Day Geisha workshop and Domestic Goddess Society classes, I go deep into the details of how to do this, but it starts with permitting yourself to actually FEEL your feelings.

For most women, anger and joy are the two easiest emotions to access. When you are used to suppressing the feelings that you deem "bad" or "negative," it's easier to express those two emotions because they feel comfortable. Often, however, there are a myriad of other emotions beneath the surface.

Your Internal GPS

Your feelings are your internal GPS, helping you navigate this existence. Being a feminine woman is all about being emotional and in tune with your emotions. Understanding your emotions and learning how to express them is a key part of feminine energy flow.

As some of you may know, I speak Spanish. I do not consider myself fluent, but I am quite functional. I really love the Spanish language because of how expressive it is, and I actually prefer speaking Spanish to English because of the language's passionate and emotional nature. There are many more word choices to precisely describe how you are feeling. I truly believe that one reason we are so out of tune with our emotions and have communication problems in relationships is due in part to the language we speak (but that's an entirely different discussion). So let's take a look at some emotions in our English language. I've compiled a list of emotions to help you navigate your feelings better. Having the names of emotions will help you more concisely express your sentiments without judging them as "good" or "bad."

PLEASANT FEELINGS

HAPPINESS:
Happy
Great
Good
Thankful
Delighted
Overjoyed
Gleeful
Elated
Jubilant

GOOD:
Calm
Peaceful
Comfortable
Content
Relaxed
Blessed

Reassured

LOVE:
Loving
Considerate
Affectionate
Tender
Attracted
Passionate
Touched
Warm

POSITIVE:
Eager
Keen
Earnest
Enthusiastic
Excited
Optimistic
Hopeful

DIFFICULT EMOTIONS

ANGER:
Irritated
Enraged
Annoyed
Upset
Unpleasant
Bitter

Offended
Aggressive
Resentful
Infuriated
Indignant

DEPRESSED:
Lousy
Disappointed
Discouraged
Ashamed
Powerless
Diminished
Guilty
Dissatisfied
Miserable
Disgusting
Bad

HURT:
Crushed
Tormented
Deprived
Pained
Rejected
Offended
Afflicted
Brokenhearted
Humiliated
Appalled

AFRAID:
Fearful
Terrified
Suspicious
Anxious
Panicked
Scared
Worried
Frightened
Threatened
Shaky
Nervous

Now that you have words to articulate your feelings, it is important to know where you are feeling them in your body. This awareness will help you constantly stay connected to your feminine energy and help you express yourself when you need to. I have included a body/emotion awareness chart to help familiarize yourself with where you are most likely to feel certain emotions in your body.

Chakra	Root	Spleen	Solar Plexus	Heart	Throat	Brow	Crown
Location	Coccyx, Perineum	Lower Abdomen	Solar Plexus Stomach	Centre of Chest	Throat	Forehead	Top of Head
Colour	Red	Orange	Yellow	Green	Blue	Indigo	Violet
Psychological Functions	Survival, Vitality, Reality, Grounding, Security, Support, Stability, Sexuality, Individuality, Courage, Impulsiveness	Feelings, Emotions, Intimacy, Procreation, Polarity, Sensuality, Confidence, Sociability, Freedom, Movement	Personal Power, Will, Knowledge, Wit, Laughter, Mental Clarity, Humor, Optimism, Self-Control, Curiosity, Awareness	Relationships, Love, Acceptance, Self-Control, Compassion, Guilt, Forgiveness, Harmony, Peace, Renewal, Growth	Communication, Wisdom, Speech, Trust, Creative Expression, Planning, Spatial, Organization, Caution	Intuition, Invention, Psychic Abilities, Self Realization, Perception, Release, Understanding, Memory, Fearlessness	Knowingness, Wisdom, Inspiration, Charisma, Awareness, Higher Self, Meditation, Self Sacrificing, Visionary
Emotions	Passions	Emotions, Desires	Purpose, Sunshine	Balance, Love	Expansion, Healing	Imagination, Intuition	Bliss, Spirituality
Glands	Adrenals	Gonads	Pancreas	Thymus	Thyroid	Pituitary	Pineal
Associated Body Parts	Spine (Chi, Life Force) Legs, Feet, Bones, Teeth, Large Intestines, Prostate, Bladder, Blood, Circulation, Tailbone	Ovaries, Testes, Womb, Kidneys, Urinary Tract, Skin, Spleen, Gallbladder, Recharges Etheric Body/Aura	Digestion, Liver, Stomach, Diaphragm, Nervous System, Pancreas, Metabolism, Small Intestines	Lungs, Heart, Bronchia, Thymus Gland, Arms, Hands, Respiratory, Hypertension, Muscles	Throat, Vocal System, Mouth, Jaw, Parathyroid, Tongue, Neck, Shoulders, Lymphs (Perspiration), Atlas, Menstrual Cycle	Eyes, Nose, Ears, Sinuses, Cerebellum, Pineal, Forebrain, Autonomic Nervous System, Heals Etheric Body/Aura	Upper brain, Cerebral Cortex, Cerebrum, Pituitary, Central Nervous System, Hair Growth, Top of Head
Physical Disfunction	Anemia, Fatigue, Obesity, Anus, Rectum (hemorrhoids), Constipation, Colds, Body Temperature, Bladder Infection, Rebuilds Blood Cells & Haemoglobin, Sciatic, Numbness, Leukemia	Impotence, Frigidity, Ovaries, Uterine Problems, Candida, Eating Disorders, Drug Use, Depression, Alcoholism, Polarity Imbalances, Gout, Allergies, Asthma (Oxygen Deficiencies)	Ulcers, Diabetes, Hepatitis, Hypoglycemia, Blood Sugar Disorders, Constipation, Nervousness, Timidity, Addictions to Stimulants, Parasites & Worms, Toxicity, Jaundice, Poor Memory	High Blood Pressure, Passiveness, Lethargy, Asthma, Immune System, Breathing Difficulties, Pneumonia, Emphysema, Cell Growth, Muscle Tension, Heart Problems, Chest Pain	Thyroid, Flu, Fevers, Blisters, Infections, Herpes, Itching, Sores, Tonsillitis, Toothaches, OCD, Speech Disorders, TMJ, Hyperactivity, Melancholy, Hormonal Problems, Swelling, Hiccups, PMS, Mood Swings	Blindness, Vision, Headaches, Migraines, Earaches, Nightmares, Sleep Disorders, Fear, Manic Depression, Anxiety, Schizophrenia, Paranoia, Equilibrium Imbalances	Depression, Alienation, Mental Illness, Neuralgia, Confusion, Senility, Veins, Blood Vessels, Lymphatic System, Bacteria, Warts, Skin Rashes, Eczema

Chart from msaprilshowers.com

Being emotionally vulnerable is the absolute only way you can have authentic connections with others AND also be authentically feminine. When it comes to our love lives, this is even truer. You absolutely MUST be emotionally available and emotionally vulnerable to maintain the yin/yang harmony of the relationship and keep your man connected.

Men are not as in tune with their feelings as we are, and when a man encounters a woman who is comfortable

65

with all of her emotions, both the pleasant and difficult ones, and who can communicate them without acting crazy, he feels safe to open up and talk. Men need us to be emotionally vulnerable and non-judgmental to consider us a safe zone, a refuge from their tough, rough, manly world.

Below is a meditation I created when I was working on expanding my heart to make room to love another man after my very painful divorce. I created this exercise to help visualize and feel what it would be like to receive pure love. I hope this will help your heart to expand as well. When doing this meditational exercise, I recommend you keep a notepad and pen nearby so you can write down any feelings that come up for you during the visualization/meditation. Any difficult feelings that pop up are things you need to work on.

I recommend doing this in a quiet space. The time of day doesn't matter at all. You can light candles or incense if you choose, but they aren't necessary.

Meditation/Visualization:

Close your eyes. You can lay back or stand.

Imagine yourself standing before the man of your dreams or your husband.
Imagine that you are completely naked. Now take your arms and stretch them out wide. The palms of your hands are turned facing him and your fingertips are stretched out.

Now imagine that he is looking at you intently with loving, warm eyes.

He can see all of you, both inside and out. He can see all of your flaws, all of your imperfections, all of your stretch marks, any scars, all of you

Imagine now that streams of pure white light are emitting from his body, and you are fully open to receive this light. Your heart area is wide open and uncovered. You can feel the light. The light feels warm, it feels good. The light is love.

How did this make you feel? What emotions came up for you? Did you feel comfortable or uncomfortable imagining yourself standing naked in front of a man who loves you for you? Explore any emotions that came up during this process. Repeat it often to gauge how open you are, and how comfortable with receiving love.

Often we say we want to experience high levels of love, but we don't know exactly what that would feel like. If we want to experience real love, we must, at the very least, have a notion of what that could possibly feel like.

I know you may be in a situation where you don't feel like you can trust anyone. You may think men are horrible. You may have been used and abused, but my dear, sweet sister, you must heal. If you do not heal and become emotionally vulnerable, you won't experience the fullness of love and you will make yourself a target for being used for sex by men (this is the hard truth). If a man can't have your heart, he may try to use you for your body.

Open your heart. Open your soul. Experience love!

11. Take Care of You

Women should not have to adopt masculine traits in order to succeed. You should be able to stay as a woman, and in tune with your femininity, and still be equal. - Isla Fisher

Now that you have taken off your cape, your heart is expanding. You are feeling brand new and it's time to take care of YOU, my sweets!

Self-care is an expression of love. We all know you can't properly love on other people if you are continuously neglecting yourself.

Create a Beauty Ritual

When I think of beauty rituals, my mind is transported to ancient Egypt. The ancient Egyptians were devoted to having daily beauty rituals, and smelling good was very important. They were famous for their perfume oils. My mind is even taken to the enslavement period of our ancestors, when African-American women used time off on Sundays to beautify themselves and get creative by grooming their hair in elaborate styles and dyeing their clothing different colors.

Looking good has always been important to us. It was said that "in 1744 in South Carolina, members of a grand jury responded to black women who did NOT obey legal clothing restrictions, by complaining that 'Negro women in particular do not restrain themselves in the clothing as the law requires, but dress in apparel quite gay and beyond their station''' (Encyclopedia of African-American History, 1619-1895, books.google.com). No law has ever, or will ever, stop us from looking fabulous; this is who we are! Looking good and beautifying ourselves is our tradition, so now we only have to make it a priority in our lives!

I encourage you to create a simple daily beauty routine to keep your skin (both face and body), teeth, hair, and nails looking healthy and beautiful. Once a week, I suggest you take time to do a more intricate beauty ritual, like a ritual bath with candles, music, bath salts, oils, whatever it is that gets you in your juicy, feminine, sensual flow. Afterwards, I recommend you rub yourself down with shea butter or anoint your own body with rich oils. Take your time and do not rush any step of this process. Take the time to hear yourself breathe, feel your heart beat, and feel your body.

Let your entire family know this is your practice. This is how you take care of you so that you can love them better. During this time, there should be NO interruptions. Let your family know that you simply cannot be interrupted during this time (except for an obvious emergency).

Then, once a month after your monthly period, I suggest doing something to pamper yourself and cleanse your body. Drink a special tea (my favorite is Healthy

Cycle by Traditional Medicinal, and Kava Stress Relief by Yogi teas), do a yoni steam, something to show your body appreciation for being a part of the beautiful reproductive cycle, for being a woman.

You can also do a special bath for your daughter during her menses. I love doing lavender baths for my daughter during her period. I got this idea from an acquaintance of mine. I serve her a special tea and chocolates, wash her locs, and baby her. I encourage you to have your family treat you delicately during your period as well; after all, you are carrying the family jewels – your eggs!

12. Makeup

A girl should be two things: classy and fabulous.
- Coco Chanel

In this day and age of YouTube tutorials, lash extensions, and brows on FLEEK, having one's face beat has become the norm. We've all seen one or two miracle contour videos that have left us speechless.

I don't feel comfortable telling women exactly how much makeup to wear, but I will say this about the subject: less is best. Makeup should enhance your beauty and features, not transform you into an entirely different person. If you are going to wear lash extensions, please make sure they are natural looking and high quality, and for the love of God, PLEASE, I beg you, stop going to these little nail shops and getting those individual lashes with the glue piled on them. My dear sweet sister, honestly, it looks tacky and classless, like a tarantula spider crawled on your eyes and died. It wouldn't be right of me if I didn't tell you the truth.

Brows should be groomed with a nice arch, and somewhat full (pencil-thin brows are not in at the time of this writing). If you use concealer to enhance them, please blend well so the concealer doesn't show on the top.

I normally look at the wives of presidents, royalty, and dignitaries as examples of how a high-value, high-status woman wears her makeup. First Lady Michelle

Obama is an excellent example. She wears makeup, but she never looks overdone, just pretty and polished.

I would also like to mention that most high value men do not find a lot of makeup attractive on a woman. Many men think that a woman who wears excessive makeup is hiding something or insecure about herself. Something to think about if you are wanting to attract a high value man.

13. Mental Health

So I'm not worried about the emotions I carry with me, because I'm happy that I have them; I think it's good for the work I do. The emotions that are not healthy are the ones you hold inside, like anger.
- Diana Ross

As all of you may or may not know that at this point, a few years ago, after my divorce, I suffered a very serious emotional breakdown. I struggled to regain a sense of self, of normalcy, and to happiness again. My faith crumbled. My religious foundation was shattered, and I lost almost all my hope. My only motivation to get right was my daughter, who is autistic. She needed me to be right.

I didn't want to take prescribed anti-depressants, but I knew I needed something because I seriously believe that, due to emotional stress, my brain had been rewired. After some research, I started taking a combination of 5-HTP, Zenta, and Kava Root pills. This totally changed my life because the 5-HTP in particular triggers the brain to secrete serotonin, a chemical that is naturally released when you are happy. I suggest talking to your doctor, mental health provider, or homeopathic practitioner about taking it.

The mental health of black women is something that needs more dialogue because although we say we are strong, we suffer from depression and mental illness more than any other group of women in this country. I think this is another reason why I reject the label "strong black woman" and prefer the term "resilient," because so many of my sisters feel they have to live up to that title and are suffering dearly as a result.

We are women. We are to be treated gently and handled with care, yet we have the ability to bounce back into shape. This is resilience, the ability to bounce back, and we do it with grand style.

If you are feeling overwhelmed and overworked, admit it. Admit to yourself you are having difficulty bearing the load. Reach out for help. Create community. If you don't have reliable family, create your own; that's what I had to do.

If you suffer from depression or bi-polar disorder, it's nothing to be ashamed of. Seek professional help, take herbal supplements, remove NEGATIVE people from your life, and take care of YOU!

14. Get Fit

"When I get up and work out, I'm working out just as much for my girls as I am for me, because I want them to see a mother who loves them dearly, who invests in them, but who also invests in herself. It's just as much about letting them know as young women that it is okay to put yourself a little higher on your priority list."
-Michelle Obama

My love, we need to have a serious conversation about the obesity issue in our community. I'll admit it, I feel a bit nervous tackling this subject due to the body shaming campaign that is going hard in this country right now, but I need to for several reasons.

Medical studies show that four out of five African-American women are obese. This is always up for debate because there's the question of whether or not this statistic is in comparison to Europeans, who have a different body type genetically.

Being "curvy" and "thick" is the "in" thing now thanks to celebrities like Jennifer Lopez and Kim Kardashian (even though her curves are bought). They helped white America embrace a fuller body shape. However, there is a big difference between being thick and being obese, out of shape, and at risk for diabetes, cancer, heart attacks, and a poor quality of life. There is a difference between having curvy hips and thighs and not being able to climb a flight of stairs because your knees and back hurt.

Then there's the issue of being overweight and male attraction. Yes, I said it, and I have said it with love, but it's time we address all of these issues honestly and with love and care.

There are many contributing factors as to why black women are leading in the area of obesity. I feel there is also a correlation between high obesity rates, high rates of depression, and high rates of singletons.

Our health is the number-one reason we need to get fit. If we are not in good health and living at optimal levels, we simply cannot achieve generational excellence. To have strong families and love lives, we simply must be of sound mind and body. We've got the spiritual aspect down because nobody goes to religious services more than black women do, but we need to improve in the area of fitness, health, and nutrition. I am happy to see a growing trend of improvement in this area on social media outlets such as Instagram and Facebook; this is encouraging to me.

Many times we hold on to the cultural myth that our African genetics make us obese, but I just don't see any evidence of this. We are obese because we eat unhealthy food and are sedentary. One of the things I loved about Paris was the active lifestyle. People walked everywhere and I barely saw any obese people; even among black Parisians or Africans, I just didn't see it.

I recommend first seeking a medical evaluation to make sure you can start an exercise program, but then, start walking. Exercising is a great stress reliever and natural anti-depressant. Walking is free, and you can do it anywhere. I also suggest adding weights and stretching to your routine. Having a full range of motion will help you age better. Also get a workout buddy; working out with friends is fun and keeps you accountable.

Now to tackle the very difficult and touchy subject of weight and looking aesthetically pleasing to men. Before I dive into this subject, let me first say a few things. I am NOT saying that a big girl can't get a man. I am NOT saying that if you are overweight you are not worthy of love, nor am I saying there aren't men out there who are attracted to obese/overweight women specifically.

I have been on both ends of the spectrum. At the time of this writing I have lost nearly 90 pounds and I am about a size 12 at 5 feet 7 and a half inches tall. All this is said without malice in my heart, but rather with love because I want the best for you. I know what it feels like to struggle with being overweight. I also spend a great deal of time talking candidly to men of all races, ages, educational levels, and walks of life to better understand how and what they think about so I can better coach women.

In general (key word GENERAL), most men are attracted to women who have slender curves, fit body types, fit thick body types, or curvy body types (especially men of color), and this is for several reasons. Men are visual; the truth is that when a man approaches a woman, it is because she has first stimulated his interest visually. Also, men are genetically hardwired to seek physically healthy women with whom to reproduce, so there is a subconscious association they make with a woman's level of health and ability to reproduce.

Upon meeting a woman, a man needs only a few minutes to decide whether or not he is physically attracted to her, and whether or not the woman is the kind of woman who would fit into his world. As a woman, the more attractive your body shape, the higher your chance of getting multiple suitors.

Living in Latin culture, I can say that Latinas (in general) care about staying in shape, and they are not ashamed to say that one reason they stay in shape is to keep their man attracted to them. In Brazil in particular, the women are shameless about the need to look sexy and to stay youthful and good looking for themselves AND their men. Looking good is extremely important in their culture.

Many men say that excess weight gain is a turn off to them, and a deterrent when it comes to marriage. You see, my dear, a man wants to feel sexually attracted to his woman. If he's going to give up all his options (even though he doesn't have as many "options" as he thinks he has), and to have sex with one woman for the rest of his life, he wants to know that she cares enough to stay attractive, and he wants to feel attracted to her. When I talk to men candidly, this fear comes up a lot! Men are sexually stimulated visually, and that's how their penises function.

In our culture, women have bought into the idea that men should be "mature" and not think about things like weight, or not care if their wife has put on an excess amount, that he should focus on the inside. "He should just love me the way I am," many women say, but remember, men and women are EQUAL but DIFFERENT. Now, of course, physical looks aren't the only thing, and yes, who you are as a person does count, as does your confidence level, but when you understand male psychology and how men are genetically hardwired to compete with other men for resources, food and women, you will understand that a man naturally wants the absolute best woman he can get. A man's social status and how he is rated and respected by other men can be affected by the type of woman he has, and how she behaves and looks.

Most men dare not mention anything about this subject for fear that saying anything will cause an argument. Men have been trained to be politically correct when it comes to this topic, but when asked to speak candidly or in the company of other men, this is what they are saying.

Think of the age-old question: "Do these jeans make me look fat?" Men know this is a trick question; they know that even if those jeans really do make you look fat, the correct answer is, "Baby, you look great in those jeans." I'll add this, however: At the very least, it should be your goal to maintain the same body shape you had when you first got together. Even if you have children, this is possible.

I was in a sexless marriage in my early 30s. My ex-husband, in a nice way, openly admitted that my weight gain was one of the reasons he no longer felt sexually attracted to me (although there were other factors, too). I knew I had put on some pounds, but I felt good. I still felt sexy. However, at the end of the day I wasn't the one looking at me, and it wasn't until the end of our marriage and I started taking pictures that I realized how much weight I had put on. I actually started studying the science and psychology of male attraction after suffering in a sexless marriage.

So I encourage you, for your health, your husband/future husband, and the generational excellence of your family, to get fit! Please don't shoot the messenger. I realize you may feel upset after reading this. It may feel like people are always saying something negative about black women, but this is not an attack, simply a loving reminder that this is an area of improvement. We are fabulous, but we can do better in a few areas.

15. What to Do with Your Money

"Black women were created of
brown sugar and warm honey.
the sweetest thing to bless the earth.
be wary of anyone who tells you otherwise."
— *Alexandra Elle*

Here's a hint: It's not paying bills. In today's modern society, nothing pushes people's emotional buttons like the topic of money. Money is the root of all evil, or so they say. Also, because more women are making just as much, if not more, money than some men (especially in our community) and gender roles are becoming blurred, the question as to who pays what and when can be just plain confusing.

Black women, according to recent polls, are officially the most educated group of people in the country, period. Across gender and racial lines, we are the most educated. We are also the fastest growing group of entrepreneurs in the country. Let's face it, most of us are doing our own thing, making our own money, and doing it well, but let's be clear about one thing. We are NOT providers. We are NOT men. Men are providers.

You may be in a position where you have to do what you must for the sake of your children, or perhaps you are single and very financially successful, or maybe you are married and both you and your spouse work long hours to contribute to your current lifestyle. Still, you are not a provider. Men are genetically hardwired to work, provide, protect, and procreate, and when you have a man, you should let him do just that.

"To understand who men are, what they have in common, and why men struggle to prove their worth to each other, reduce male groups to their nucleic form. Sprawling, complex civilizations made up of millions of people are relatively new to men. For most of their time on this planet, men have organized small survival bands, set against hostile environment, competing for women and resources with other bands of men. Understanding the way men react to each other demands an understanding of their most basic social unit. Understanding what men want from each other requires an understanding of what men have most often needed from each other, and a sense of how these needs have shaped masculine psychology." (Way of Men, Jack Donovan pg. 78)

Men have an actual need to provide and be seen as competent within the group of men he associates with. By helping him with his role, it actually suppresses his instincts to take care of you.

Taking care of a man, splitting bills, and buying things for him (on a regular basis) emasculates him. It also makes you look like less of a woman in his eyes, as he no longer sees you as a feminine woman who needs his provision or protection. Doing so can attract users, abusers, and losers. We deserve more than that, my love.

On Dates

As a rule of thumb, a woman should NEVER pay for a date (even a date with her husband) unless it is the man's birthday, a special occasion, or a holiday. Why? Because a man paying for the date is an important part of the courtship process, demonstrating that he is both willing and able to be a provider. Once married, he continues to provide.

"But, Candice, what if he's a little tight one week and I really want to go to that steak house? Why should I deprive myself?" If he can't afford something that week, I suggest being humble and doing something free or within his budget. Do not pay. Men value humility, and that is a top quality when they seek a wife. A woman paying is exerting her masculine energy (because masculine energy is about doing), and you always want to be ultra-feminine with your guy. Men feel manlier when they are providers and protecting.

At Home, Bills, and Other Things

So, what can your money go towards? Your money can go towards anything outside of basic necessities. You are a prize, so no taking care of men!

If you are single, when in the dating phase it should be negotiated that your money will not be used for household bills. Expressing your desire and expectation to be provided for will not be a turn-off for a healthy, masculine man.

Below is a short list of what your money can go towards to benefit your family.

1.) College funds
2.) Personal care, gym membership, personal trainer
3.) Family vacations
4.) Starting a family business
5.) Trust funds
6.) Emergency funds

The bottom line is that a woman who knows that she is ultra-feminine and a prize understands it is to her advantage to not foot any bills. You are a queen and should be treated as such.

16. Develop YOUR Creativity, Ideas, Skills, and Talents

Sometimes you have to let everything go - purge yourself. If you are unhappy with anything - whatever is bringing you down - get rid of it. Because you will find that when you are free, your true creativity, your true self comes out.
- Tina Turner

Feminine energy is creative, innovative energy. As women, we are powerful creators because we are the more spiritually in tune of the two genders. Our ability to create and to manifest is very strong.

Take the time to find out what your passions are. What do you do that makes you feel amazingly good whenever you do it? Take classes, learn languages, and find creative ways to make money.

1)Paint
2)Take a salsa or kizomba dance class
3)Write a book
4)Organize a family photo album or scrapbook

5)Plan a language abroad trip
6)Learn to sew
7)Write and perform a play with your family
8)Organize a community bake sale
9)Make a list of everything you love to do
10)Learn one new recipe each month

17. Mastermind Groups

"My complexion had always been an obstacle to overcome and all of a sudden, Oprah was telling me it wasn't. It was perplexing and I wanted to reject it because I had begun to enjoy the seduction of inadequacy. But a flower couldn't help but bloom inside of me...."
-Lupita Nyong'o

Start a mastermind group with other feminine women to create ideas together and exchange knowledge. Multiple intelligent minds working and creating together are better than one single mind.

All the wealthy people and progressive people throughout time have been part of a mastermind group. Building this type of community is essential to the healing of our community.

18. Knowledge is Power

"The way black women say "girl" can be magical. Frankly, I have no solid beliefs about the survival of consciousness after physical death. But if it's going to happen I know what I want to see after my trek toward the light. I want to see a black woman who will smile and say, "Girl...."
— *Abigail Padgett, Blue*

Take history classes, reading and literature classes, financial classes, art classes, music lessons, voice lessons, creative writing classes, and cooking classes. Take time to discover math, science, and budgeting classes. You never know what hidden talents lie dormant if you don't develop them.

It is important to be a well-rounded lady. A feminine lady is no dummy. These skills and talents will make you interesting, a valuable wife, and set you apart from other women who are…
well…simply put, basic. Not only this, your knowledge is something that can be taught to your children and grandchildren. A mother is a child's first teacher.

19. Be a Freak in the Sheets

I am sensual and very physical. I'm very erotic. But my sexuality exists on a sort of a fantasy level.

-Donna Summer

Everyone knows that a man wants a lady in the streets and a freak in the sheets. A blissfully feminine woman knows how to do both well!

With respect to the subject of sex, if you are a marriage-minded single woman, I HIGHLY suggest you not have sex with a man until engagement or marriage. If you want to maintain the perception that you are high value, this is what I suggest. I explain the reasons in greater detail in my Intentional Dating Program. I know that many of you are having sex without a ring or any sign of a formal commitment, but I'd feel irresponsible if I didn't let you know, my dear.

Blow Jobs

1.) So, let's get to it. A blow job, my dear, is the number-one most requested sex act by men. Men love to receive blow jobs mostly because of how much it increases their masculinity. Because feminine vulnerability is such a turn-on for men, a woman on her knees with his penis in her mouth is probably one of the most vulnerable sexual positions a woman can be in.

To Swallow or Not to Swallow: That Is the Question

I personally think that you should swallow if your man cums in your mouth. It is a BIG way to show you fully accept him. If you just cannot stomach the thought of swallowing semen, have a pretty, feminine-looking handkerchief handy and DISCREETLY spit it out without making a bad face or comment.

For those of you who detest giving blow jobs because you think it tastes nasty or you don't like the smell, I recommend using things like flavored oral sex gels that taste like strawberries or chocolate. You can even use actual chocolate syrup. Create a sexual ritual in which you clean your man's penis. Make it fun and sensual. Whatever you do, do not deny your man this pleasure.

If you simply suck at sucking dick, search your area for sensual arts classes and learn. I know that here in my area there are classes. We also teach free sensual arts classes for members of our Domestic Goddess Society. Also, there's a great video on YouTube about using a grapefruit while giving a blow job, which is supposed to feel amazing for him. Of course, you can try using gag reflex gels and sprays for blow jobs so that you can take all of him. So girl, get on your knees!

2.) Be open to trying new positions, role playing, and incorporating toys. Be willing to experience new things can keep your relationship fresh, create deeper levels of trust, and improve communication.

3.) Add sensual massage to your foreplay, or use sensual massage as a teaser to build up sexual tension.

4.) Sacred Masturbation- For many, due to religious beliefs, masturbation is taboo. I believe that masturbation is not only healthy, but can help you to get to know your body better, and keeps you from having sex with the wrong person when you are having urges to have sex. An orgasm is energy, and provided that the intent is pure, comes from a place of self-love without guilt or fear, there is high spiritual awareness, and you are giving thought to the loving energy that you want to put out, and one day receive from a loving man, I see no reason to hold back. This is a helpful tool for single ladies who want to remain celibate until marriage.

During sacred masturbation, focus on your yoni (vagina). Think about all the love that you have to give, the gift of your sex, and then receiving that juicy love back. When you reach your peak point and orgasm, enjoy it. Then thank the universe for that moment of pure pleasure.

5.) Make your bedroom your private sanctuary. A feminine woman should make every effort to make sure the sacred space she shares with her man is clean, neat, and organized, that it smells good, looks pretty, and is sensual. This is not the place for piles of laundry, dirty towels, and the like.

Choose color palettes that create peace, yet stimulate passion. Make sure to have candles and fresh flowers (if your budget allows it), as well as items like Wallflowers from Bath & Body Works in earthy scents. Men are attracted to earthy scents, as it triggers their primal nature.

Your bedroom is your love den, your hideaway within your own home. With the exception of infants, children and animals should not be allowed to sleep in the bedroom at all. Many people, especially women, have an issue with this, but this is not child abuse or neglect. Training your children to respect the marital bed maintains passion. This will also help them in their future marriages. The marriage is the nucleus of the family, after all, and the sooner children learn to respect the foundation of the family in every way possible, the better everyone will be.

6.) Keep your energy high so you aren't too tired for sex. Men need sex. He needs you to be ready and into him.

So, be a total sex goddess. The gift of our sex is one of our super powers as women, so be a freak in the sheets.

20. Looking Pretty

Looking pretty is good manners. It is ill mannered to go out in public without giving care or thought as to how you look. The truth is more people have to look at you during the day, than you do, unless you are glued to the mirror 24/7.

I remember the era when our people got dressed up to go everywhere. Going to the "picture show" (movies) we got dressed up. Going to visit Aunt Sally down the road, you got dressed up. Even just hanging out because it was a Tuesday, our people got dressed up.

We desperately need to bring classy back. Seeming that we are the innovators of style and trends in this country and around the world it needs to start with us.

Now let's address another important reason to stay looking pretty. Men!

As we know, men are visual. Looking pretty for bedtime is just as important as looking pretty during the day. Tap into your sensual side by making sure to have a nice collection of lingerie and girly, frilly, feminine nightgowns to wear at night, or sleep naked, if you prefer.

Imagine that after a hard day out in the world, working hard, competing, and being drained, all your man really wants is to come home to his queen looking soft and inviting. So, no granny panties or sleeping in that free, unisex t-shirt you got at that jazz festival.

Now, I know that what I'm going to say next is going to ruffle some feathers, but I must say it. The headscarves at night are a big-time no-no. I know, I know, you are rolling your eyes at me right about now. "This girl has lost her mind," you're saying. "But my hair will be messed up in the morning," you're saying. Well, I say this: There are solutions to every issue. The truth is, going to bed looking like Harriet Tubman (God rest her soul, and we appreciate her sacrifices) is NOT sexy. It's just not sexy. Men, especially black men, accept it because they feel they have no choice and they don't want an argument. Men really don't like to argue. However, just because they accept it doesn't mean they find it sexy and that it makes their penis hard. However, when speaking candidly they do admit that they feel less sexually attracted to their partner when she wears the night bonnet or scarf to bed.

Okay, so because I am solution-oriented, below is a list of suggestions to have your edges laid in the morning.

1.) Sleep on a satin pillowcase.
2.) Wear small scarves instead of large ones that cover the entire head.

3.) Go natural; most men prefer natural hair, anyway.
4.) Wear braids.
5.) Wear wash-and-go styles.
6.) Use an edge control gel at night along with a cute, small scarf.

21. Be the Hostess with the Mostess

"She is free in her wildness, she is a wanderess, a drop of free water. She knows nothing of borders and cares nothing for rules or customs. 'Time' for her isn't something to fight against. Her life flows clean, with passion, like fresh water."
— ***Roman Payne***

Feminine women bring people together, especially family. Make it a point to plan gatherings monthly to bring family and friends together. This will create life long bonds and traditions that will easily pass onto the next generation.

Also when having house guests stay with you, there are ways that you can shine as a feminine, nurturing woman. A woman who pays attention to certain details leaves a lasting impression.

Some great ideas from bringing the people you love together:

1.) Have themed dinners.

2.) Host brunch at your house.

3.) Make sure you have clean towels and extra toiletries for you house guests, including extra toothbrushes, sanitary napkins or tampons.

4.) Always have a few extra bottles of wine both alcoholic and non-alcoholic for those who may not drink alcohol.

5.) Send an email or card in the mail to let your guests know you enjoyed having them in your home. This especially includes family.

6.) Make sure to serve your guests.

7.) Make a unique quest book with your family to have each guest that comes to your house sign, so you can remember who came to special dinners.

8.) Give a mini house tour to first time visitors.

9.) Always see your guests out upon them leaving.

10.) Always offer your guests something to drink and a snack or meal.

22. Feminine Hygiene

The pain is necessary. Sometimes pain is the teacher
we require, a hidden gift of healing and hope.
-Janet Jackson

Although I think most of us know this, it is
important to take care of your feminine hygiene. Staying
on top of your hygiene is not only healthy, but just makes
you feel better.

Also men really like for a woman to be clean not
only in her outer appearance, but also keep her body clean
and smelling good.

1.) Make sure your lady parts are clean and fresh-
smelling. Use perfume oils between your thighs (my
favorite is Egyptian Musk Oil) or an intimate spray.

2.) Keep your pubic hairs trimmed, or get a bikini or
Brazilian wax. Just an FYI, Brazilian waxes make
intercourse feel AMAZING! A side note about Brazilian
waxes. There is a lot of debate about how hygienic they
really are. I used to get them regularly, but now, I prefer to
keep some hair down there. I get deep bikini waxes and
trim low.

3.) Bathe regularly and take two baths or showers
daily.

4.) Avoid douching

5.) Use menstrual cups instead of tampons or use
organic sanitary napkins or tampons

6.) Use all natural deodorant and feminine wash

7.) Get a yoni steam. Yoni steaming is an ancient tribal practice that helps soothe and revitalize the interior of your vagina. The vagina is self-cleaning, however yoni steaming feels good, can help reduce pain and bloating from menstruation, assist in the healing of vaginal tears postpartum, and even relieve vaginal dryness which can cause pain during sexual intercourse.

Be sure to talk to your doctor if you have any questions about how yoni steaming will affect your health, and make sure to find a reputable place to go for this service. You can also purchase yoni steaming chairs and herbs only and do them at home!

The Jamaican model Nerissa Irving has some great vegan and organic feminine hygiene products on her website www.shop.nerissairving.com. Her goal is to save one pum pum at a time!

23. Authentic Femininity

Don't settle for average. Bring your best to the moment. Then, whether it fails or succeeds, at least you know you gave all you had. We need to live the best that's in us.
-Angela Bassett

Being authentically feminine is important. Being authentic as a human is important, period. Being authentically feminine is your ability to thoroughly enjoy your existence as a woman who is thriving in the full force of her feminine energy.

Man-charming is <u>not</u> authentic femininity. It is a component of being girly, fun, and feminine, but using femininity as a means of getting a husband is, in my opinion, underhanded and mean. Besides, a man can and will eventually realize you are a fraud. You can't attract or keep a good, high-quality, emotionally healthy, masculine man without being authentically feminine.

My own femininity has unfolded in stages. I was not always comfortable being girly, juicy, sensual, and feminine. In fact, girls who were naturally this way used to irritate me. I went through my tomboy phase, and I went through my phase in which I thought that just because I loved to wear makeup and high heels, I was "feminine." It is only now that I can say I fully understand and enjoy being a woman and being feminine. I embrace my essence as a feminine soul. I am absolutely enamored with being female, with being a lady.

As you grow on this journey to becoming authentically feminine, be gentle with yourself. Some things may feel strange, but just like starting a new workout regime, with time your practice as a woman will become a habit and it will feel normal to be blissfully feminine!

24. Be Girly, Not Grown

I know who I am. I am not perfect.

I'm not the most beautiful woman in the world. But I'm one of them.

-Mary J. Blige

Black women love to remind people that they are grown. "Um, excuse me, I am not one of these little girls. I'm grown." How many times have we heard this? "We don't play no games, we don't take no mess. We handle our business and we won't be entertained by anyone who dares to try our 'grownness.'" This attitude is prevalent in our community. I get it; you want to be taken seriously, but, my lovely sister, this demeanor keeps you stuck in a masculine energy zone. It is a wall that keeps you from just being girly and free.

Men desire a woman who is soft, free, fun, and girly, not "grown." This doesn't mean you are irresponsible, but that you are well-balanced and don't take yourself too seriously. The more masculine a man is, the more he will crave a soft, feminine woman as his counterpart. The yin to his yang.

Being grown may serve you well in the boardroom, the classroom, or the courtroom, but outside of that, you should strive to tap into your fun, girly energy. Being girly will keep your stress levels low, as well as make you more appealing to men and just more pleasant to be around. A good attitude is a key factor that men look for when choosing a wife. "Having a good temperament makes you more attractive and alluring as a woman. That basically means having traits of personality that makes you a good companion to live with, and certain personality traits that are harmonious to each other." (www.thefemininebelle.com)

Some of these girly and harmonious traits are:

Friendliness
Positivity/cheerfulness
Energy
Playfulness

A few things you can do to get in a girly and energetic mood:

Laugh
Let your hair down (literally)
Play; yes, actually play, jump rope, swing on a swing, play hide and seek
Dance

25. Be Nice to Men

I've come to the conclusion that beautiful women in the West aren't comfortable finding strength in their femininity. They want to do masculine-oriented things to establish their femininity. It's a contradiction.
-Wesley Snipes

In my travels and while mingling with other cultures, I have noticed a stark difference between how the genders interact with each other. I especially love the way Latin men and women interact. There is always a playful, sometimes flirty exchange that goes on between the sexes, even if it's a casual interaction. The culture allows one to enjoy the seduction that goes on between men and women. Women enjoy the company of men, and men enjoy the attention of women. It's fun and the energy exchange is appreciated.

Not so much in American culture. We tend to find men annoying. A stank face and "Ugh, why is he talking to me?" are common responses to men who try to approach women. Or if a guy walks up to a woman and asks for her name, the response for many would be, "Why do you want to know my name?" or some other rude reply. Or a guy will approach a group of ladies and get dogged. I've seen this far too many times and it makes me sad. It makes me sad because behaviors like this give us a reputation for being mean, and I know that deep down we aren't really mean.

As we grow in our femininity, as we are come to understand the powerful influence of our feminine energy, it is so vital that we grasp the way we treat everyone around us, including men, matters. Men are using the information we give them both verbally and non-verbally to determine how to treat us, how to make us happy, and how to categorize us into their lives.

Men and women are equal but different, and men feed off our energy in a unique way. Learn to use everyday interactions with men to appreciate their masculinity and the importance they play in your life. I find, in most instances, men are starving for our feminine energy and nurturing.

I know this may be a difficult hurdle, as many black women in America don't have positive examples of men and women flowing together in yin/yang harmony. You may currently believe that men are bad, are dogs, users, and abusers.

Perhaps your father wasn't around (70% of African Americans grow up without a father in the home), or if he was around, maybe he wasn't taking care of his masculine duties or he was abusive. Maybe your mother was more masculine in her energy, and was verbally aggressive to all the men in her life. Or perhaps you have a history of dealing with men who have used you for sex, money, or both, or maybe you have baby daddy drama going on and feel that because of your experience, men don't deserve to be treated nicely.

The modern-day feminist movement has done a lot of good in certain areas of women's rights, but has done a lot of damage in causing a divide in this area, pitting women against men. Just because this is your history and current point of attraction doesn't mean it has to be your legacy. You can change, and it is imperative to your family's generational excellence as well as our community as African descendants living in America that we do.

Emasculating men and treating them like children has become common in our society. From movies like *Straight Outta Compton* to The Real Housewives series, we see women emasculating men both verbally and physically. The loud, mean, aggressive, emasculating image is what is portrayed and even celebrated in our community, but it is extremely damaging. Men NEED high levels of respect to feel properly and thoroughly loved. Their need for respect, again, comes from their genetic programming to compete with other men for food, resources, and women. Typically, the men who receive the highest levels of respect from both men and women are considered leaders and have better opportunities for resources and financial gain (*The Way of Men*). This is one of the main reasons it is so damaging when a woman is rude and disrespectful to her man.

Here are five tips you can incorporate into your daily practice to be nice to men, to appreciate their masculine energy, and to polish your femininity. These daily practices will dramatically help change the way you view and relate to men (regardless of your relationship to them), and how they respond to you as a woman.

1.) Flirt. The art of flirting – as I have learned from a mentor of mine, Stacey Murphy – is nothing more than making another person feel good for the sake of making them feel good. Flirting doesn't have to be over the top or sexually oriented. One easy way to flirt is by paying compliments. "Hey, handsome" or "That suit makes you look so distinguished" are a great start. We compliment women so easily – "Oh, girl, you are killing it in that dress" – but men rarely get compliments, so this will be greatly appreciated.

2.) Show appreciation. Men live to please us; the appreciation is the gas they need in their tanks to keep doing more. Thank them and brag on them in public. Make a big deal out of little things.

3.) Ask for help. I've said it a few times in this book, and I'm saying it again. Men need to feel needed, so ask for help. Even if you can do it for yourself, if a man is present, let him do it for you.

4.) Be nice to men when they approach you. If you are even fairly decent-looking, men will try to talk to you, as they are genetically hardwired to pursue women. This is normal, natural male behavior that should not annoy you.

Even if you aren't interested, suppress the need to be rude. Let them down easily and with a smile. Learn to appreciate the small form of adoration, even if it's from a man to whom you may not be attracted. It's not going to kill you to chat it up and be nice for a few minutes.

5.) Speak positively about men. Avoid conversations with other women in which you trash-talk men. By speaking positively of men, you will attract more positive interactions with them.

Men are not our enemies. We need each other for balance. There is power in our feminine presence. High-quality, feminine women are nice to men. A genuinely nice personality is a quality that men seek in a wife.

26. Act Like a Lady, Get Treated Like a Queen

Why can't women get along? Because we're afraid.
We're afraid to be vulnerable. We're afraid to be soft.
We're afraid to be hurt. But most of all, we're afraid of our
power. So we become controlling and aggressive and
vicious.
-Iyanla Vanzant

With so many contradictory messages in our culture, modern women are confused about what being a lady actually means. Since the start of the modern feminist movement in the 1960's, women have been encouraged to be competitive and career oriented. (There is nothing wrong with having career goals.)

Do we think like a man? Act like one of the guys? Is it okay to burp and fart in front of guys? The confusion can honestly make one's head spin.

The truth is this: Masculine men deeply desire with all of their hearts a soft, delicate, feminine woman. This doesn't mean that you have to dumb yourself down or be docile, but you do have to act like a lady.

Act like a lady and you will get treated like a queen. Every manly man wants that one special woman whom he can call his queen, whom he can protect. When selecting a wife, a high-quality, masculine man will go after only his polar opposite: a classy, feminine lady.

1.) You are not one of the boys. Even though it may be tempting, refrain from behaving like one of the boys. If you want to continuously stimulate the masculine instinct of the men around you to protect you, take care of you, and treat you delicately, don't start this habit. Avoiding masculine behavior like burping and farting in front of guys, sitting with your legs open, talking loudly, and cursing will also keep you from getting friend-zoned by high-quality men.

2.) Be the most feminine woman in the room. Whenever you enter a room, infuse it with your feminine essence. Give out hugs, smiles, and loving looks. Be an attentive listener. Learn the art of conversation.

3.) Dress like a lady. American culture has gotten extremely casual. The days when people took the time and effort to look nice for themselves and others in their presence everywhere they went are long gone. We needn't look farther than our local Super Walmart to see this. However, we can bring classy back! I encourage you to wear more dresses, as dresses are the most feminine – not to mention the easiest – thing a woman can wear.

I love the days of Dorothy Dandridge and Lena Horne, when ladies were just so classy and fabulous. They are my inspiration. Strive to be classy and lady-like. Bypass the Instagram boutiques and avoid the trend of dressing like a high-class call girl or stripper. (Doing so will make you a target for being used for sex or put in the sex-only category by men...)

4.) Be gentle and soft. Everything about you should be soft and gentle. Your voice, your hand movements, the way you get in and out of your chair or car. You are like water and air. Wear fabrics that are soft and that feel good on you.

5.) Avoid harsh talking, gossiping, and cursing/using bad words, especially in front of men. Protect your femininity – it's yours!

6.) Learn proper table etiquette and work diligently to refine your manners. A high-quality man especially loves a classy, feminine woman whom he can take anywhere and who won't embarrass him in public. Men who have high-status careers in particular need a woman who can mingle with people from different social statuses.

When you act like a lady, you will get treated like a lady. You will draw a certain type of man to you.

Throw away the notion that you could even think like a man. You should strive to understand men more, to refine yourself as a woman, to be the best you can be personally, and to be the best wife you can be. Being a fun, classy lady is what will separate you from the bunch.

7.) Be interesting and speak your mind. A lady knows when to say something, what to say, how to say it, and when to keep her mouth shut. Be interesting, read, keep yourself up to date on current events, learn about art, history, different genres of music, go to cultural events and festivals. Have a life and be genuinely interesting. Being feminine is not about not having an opinion or anything to say. It's simply a matter of knowing how to say it, and with love.

27. Be a Domestic Goddess

I've learned that people will forget what you said,
people will forget what you did,
but people will never forget how you made them feel.

~ Maya Angelo

What is a Domestic Goddess? A Domestic Goddess is a woman who understands that her personal goals and plans must be in alignment with her calling to be a wife and mother. A Domestic Goddess is a woman with a passion for life, whose heart is in the home. She understands that her feminine presence is a powerful force in her home that will not only affect those living with her, but will touch the lives of many living outside the walls of her home, as well as future generations.

A Domestic Goddess understands that to be effective in the home, she needs to be present in her home. She is not trying to be an overworked modern-day Superwoman/slave who has bought into the "I-can-work-40-hours-a-week-plus-overtime-and-still-have-it-all" system. She understands she can have a full, rewarding life, but her priorities and the way she divides her time will look much different from the average woman's schedule.

Family First

This is easier said than done for most, but family must come first. If you are married, your husband must come first, before the children. So many women have an issue with this, with visions of children locked away in closets, unfed, neglected, and abused. Putting your husband first doesn't mean in an unhealthy way in which your children are neglected; it simply means you understand your marriage is the nucleus of the family and that if the marriage isn't right, the family isn't right.

As a Domestic Goddess, you are responsible for keeping your family together. Creating moments to build family bonds and memories is critical to the development of your family. Teaching your children to value family and to know that blood is thicker than water is a principal that can be passed down.

28. Educate Your Seed

I believe that children are our future. Teach them well and let them lead the way. Show them all the beauty they possess inside.
-Whitney Houston

You are responsible for educating your children. Far too often, we leave the education of our children to other people. This is ruining our communities at the root. As black people, we can no longer afford to leave our children's minds to a system that doesn't fully benefit them.

A few things on your agenda for truly educating your children should be:

1.) History (African History): Black History Month is great, but let's turn things up a notch and have Black History Year, and do it year after year because we have too much history to leave to just one month.

2.) Finances and Budgeting

3.) Morals and Values

4.) Languages: We must move toward accepting the fact we have a global society and that speaking multiple languages is an asset in so many ways.

5.) Manners and Etiquette

6.) Investing, Business, and Entrepreneurship

7.) Self-Defense: Our sons need to know how to protect the family, and our daughters need to know how to defend themselves if there is no man around.

8.) Criminal and Constitutional Law: Seeing that a higher percentage of our people end up in the criminal justice system, knowing our actual rights is a necessity.

9.) Math and Science

10.)Arts (including African Dance and drumming)

11.)Laws of Attraction (Universal Law Principles)

I am a huge advocate of home schooling, and home-school cooperatives. This is a very feminine education structure that allows children to not only learn, but be nurtured. This type of system allows a child to develop individual talents, values, and core subjects while getting the socialization that they need, and the ability to understand how a community functions.

29. Educate Yourself

You've got to learn to leave the table when love's no longer being served".
- Nina Simone

Take classes and develop your interests and talents. All of these skills can be used to pass knowledge to your children, grandchildren, and great-grandchildren, and to create extra income for your family's excellence in a feminine way.

African-American women are currently in the lead for having the most advanced degrees and education in the country, regardless of gender or race. This is a great accomplishment, and I encourage women to get higher forms of education whether formally or informally. Gain knowledge by any means necessary.

Your intellect and wisdom will make you a valuable wife, and give you an advantage over the rest when it comes to your families well-being. Knowledge is power!

30. Beautify Your Home

*In my mind, marriage is a spiritual partnership
and union in which we willingly give and receive
love, create and share intimacy, and open ourselves
to be available and accessible to another human
being in order to heal, learn and grow.*
-Iyanla Vanzant

Make sure your home is clean and inviting, and
that it smells good. Create a system to keep it from
getting cluttered. Take pride in how your home
looks. Your home is an extension of who you are; it
reflects how you feel about yourself and your
family.

1.) I suggest making your house inviting by
choosing inviting color pallets, and
strategically adding pops of bright colored
accent pieces in the room.
2.) Family pictures are a must. Have fun and
custom make unique frames for the pictures
3.) Create an at home art gallery. In my house
we have an accent wall that we have turned
into an art gallery of family paintings. When
family or friends come to visit, we will bring

out the paints and have them to create a mini masterpiece to remember them by.

4.) Display fresh flowers if your budget allows

5.) Have candles burning. Candles create such peace and tranquility, and definitely add a lot to the ambience.

31. Cook

"One cannot think well, love well, sleep well, if one has not dined well."

— Virginia Woolf

I am absolutely shocked at the number of women I meet these days who think they are going to get married to a chef or a man who likes to cook. Even if you do marry a chef or a man who loves to cook, I highly recommend you let him in your kitchen sparingly. The modern-day feminist movement has done an excellent job of making women think cooking is lowly and unnecessary.

The truth is, men get married for feminine nurturing. Cooking food is a feminine task because it is nurturing. Showing love to your family by nourishing them is important.

Meal time is a big part of creating lifelong memories. As humans, we are deeply connected to food in an emotional way. Making sure your family eats together and on time will bond your family for generations to come.

Take culinary art classes. Make meal times fun and creative. Meal time is also a great time to teach manners and etiquette. My mother always tested our manners during meal times by asking if we were we ready to meet the Queen. My mother always told us that even if a person wasn't formally educated, if they spoke grammatically correct English, were polite, and had good table manners, they could go far.

32. Be a Servant

*Let us always meet each other with smile, for
the smile is the beginning of love.*
- Mother Theresa

We were put on this earth to help build up one another, to make the world a better place to live. As a Domestic Goddess, you should have the heart of a servant, not only to love and serve your family, but to give to those outside your home. Teaching your children to serve others is a great way to kill selfishness before it has a chance to grow.

33. Volunteer

*If you find it in your heart to care
for somebody else, you will have succeeded.
-Maya Angelou*

Start a Welcome to the Neighborhood group, visit the sick, start a New Mommy group in which you cook meals for new moms during their first few weeks of being home with their babies, or call people instead of texting them. In a world of social media and texting, receiving an actual phone call feels wonderful.

I also suggest organizing a *Greet Your Precinct* group. I got this idea on Facebook after one mother decided to do something proactive and positive after a string of police shootings. She decided to take her children up to their local police precinct so that she could meet the local police officers that patrolled her neighborhood and they could get to know her children. We've actually done this in our local area, and I think this is one way that we as feminine women can create relationships and bridge communities.

These are many different ways to be effective as a Domestic Goddess. What you bring to your family, your community, and the world is so powerful. You are more than an extra paycheck, a bill payer. Your husband and children are more than accessories for your life and career. Your actual presence – mind, body, and spirit – is needed. Your calling to the Domestic Goddess Society is a beautiful and rewarding one.

34. Be Graceful

Choose people who lift you up.
-Michelle Obama

Feminine grace is probably one of my favorite parts of femininity and being a woman. To me, it's so fun to just WERK every aspect of being a woman. This is where you can have fun and incorporate your style.

Feminine Body Movement

I am a self-proclaimed professional UN-professional dancer. I have taken numerous dance classes since I was 19 years old; from salsa to Bollywood, African to Tahitian, belly dance to Afro-Cuban dance, I've done it. I just love feminine body movement. The way a woman can charm anyone through her body movements is fascinating. Get comfortable with your body and learn to move your hips and waist. Almost every dance style on the globe incorporates hip action and delicate hand-and-shoulder movement for women. The easiest way to get into your blissfully feminine state of mind is to turn on some music and move your hips!

35. Create a Signature Walk

"Elegance is a glowing inner peace. Grace is an ability to give as well as to receive and be thankful. Mystery is a hidden laugh always ready to surface! Glamour only radiates if there is a sublime courage & bravery within: glamour is like the moon; it only shines because the sun is there."
— *C. JoyBell C.*

Most people think that walking is a means to a particular destination. The Blissfully Feminine woman understands that, yes, walking is a means to a particular destination, but the difference is that she has fun walking her way to the destination. I suggest having two or three different kinds of walks.

Your flirty walk – this walk is all about feeling fabulous and getting a man's attention. Have fun, make it slow, and take a look at videos if you need help.

Your playful walk – this walk is when you are in a fun, playful mood. You can even add a skip or a little run in between. It's all about having fun.

Your Queen of Sheba walk – this walk is when you want to command the attention of everyone in the room. You are a queen, and all others must recognize this. This walk should be slow and confident, with sultry-yet-smiling eyes, arms resting to the side, and one foot placed in front of the other. You are Queen of the Nile!

With all this walking, you're going to eventually need to sit. When you do, it needs to be with style. No plopping down in a chair. Your stand-to-sit transition should be smooth. If your knees are weak (like mine…lol), gently place your hand in the center of the chair as you bend your knees, then slide into the chair gracefully. This also goes for getting in and out of a car.

Crossing your legs.

Sitting like a lady is crucial, so train yourself to keep your knees together when sitting. Many ladies have weak inner thigh muscles, making it a bit uncomfortable to keep their legs closed. Doing inner thigh exercises can make it easier. There are two types of crossed leg styles that are appropriate for a lady: Over the Knee and At the Ankle.

Again, when it comes to sitting, I normally look at the example of royalty and dignitaries, seeing how they carry themselves and emulating that. Most royalty cross their ankles when sitting.

36. No Slamming Doors

*I see myself as sexy. If you are comfortable
with it, it can be very classy and appealing.*
- Aaliyah

Doors should be gently opened and closed
with the use of two hands. A little bit of extra effort,
but it looks very graceful and soft!

Being graceful is all about making each
movement count while looking effortless. Think of
Misty Danielle Copeland, principal dancer for the
American Ballet Theatre. Her moves are powerful,
yet soft and elegant. Avoid haphazardly throwing
your body around. Make use of your space and your
body.

"Feminine grace is when a woman is truly
happy being a woman. She is comfortable with her
femininity without being overtly sexual. Feminine
grace is coming into rapport with being a woman
and loving it in every way…"
(angelfire.com/DrGary123)

Some black women who are excellent
examples of feminine grace are/were: Diana Ross,
Michelle Obama, Lena Horne, Meagan Good,
Diahann Carroll, Garcelle Beauvais, Dorothy

Dandridge, Gina Torres, Kerry Washington, Susan Taylor, and Gabrielle Union. These women stand out through their ability to exude feminine grace, softness, charm, and poise in public.

Fine-tuning your feminine grace may take some practice, but in the end it is worth it. Have fun and enjoy being a classy lady!

37. Yoni Power

"Love recognizes no barriers. It jumps hurdles, leaps fences, penetrates walls to arrive at its destination full of hope."
—Maya Angelou

"Yoni" is a Sanskrit word (from India) meaning "sacred place," for a woman's lady parts and region. And that it is. Our yoni is our sacred place, truly. It houses the family jewels. Our lovely eggs. Quoting a very wise woman I know, a woman comes to the planet with only a certain number of eggs, and once the eggs are gone, they are gone.

This makes us unique and special as women. Our eggs also respond to and carry the energy we take in and give out, which makes it crucial that we stay as feminine as possible and protect our energy. A man can make sperm, spill his sperm, and continue to make sperm well into his later years, but we cannot. Our eggs are precious, and so is our yoni.

Our yoni also houses the sacral chakra, which is the center for creating relationships, our sense of self, family, and our sexuality. Many of us forget how sacred we actually are. We get caught up in sexual relationships that do not serve us. We create sexual soul ties to people who mean us no good.

You simply cannot let just anyone near the family jewels, now can you?

Part of caring for ourselves includes deciding whom we choose to let enter our sacred place. Even if your hair is laid, your brows, lashes, and makeup are on fleek, and you always look well-groomed, you can't claim to have high self-esteem if you aren't selective about whom you are having sex with. Who a woman has sex with is one of the most important decisions she can make. Any man you have sex with could potentially be the father of your children.

A recent scientific study was done that shows that women carry the DNA of past sexual partners. "Scientists have discovered that a sizeable minority of women have Y-chromosome gene sequence in their blood. This is interesting because as you may know, Y-chromosomes are the chromosomes that belong to men…" (www.antimediaplus.com).

"An obvious answer would be from pregnancy with a male son, every woman who has been pregnant still carries cells from her fetus within her bloodstream. Cells from the pregnancy will reside within the mother's bloodstream and organs for the rest of her life. Even if the pregnancy was terminated or if there was a miscarriage these said genes would remain within the Mother." (www.antimediaplus.com)

This is all very interesting, but we have to ask the question about women who carry the Y-chromosome, but have no male children. "This called for a study (2) that was done by immunologists at the Fred Hutchinson Cancer Center in 2004. In this study they took samples from 120 women who had never had sons. They found that 21% of these women had male DNA." (www.antimediaplus.com)

"The conclusions of this study noted that the possible sources of male michrochimerism included, known pregnancies, miscarriages, vanished male twin, or sexual intercourse. This means, that through intercourse alone there is a potential for women to hold onto male genes and DNA within their organs and blood stream for their entire life!" (www.antimediaplus.com)

That's downright scary to me. If you need a reason to keep your legs closed till your king comes, this is it. The two LITERALLY become one during sex!

If we are to make any impact on our community generationally, we must take our partner selection seriously. We must put away this baby daddy foolishness, situationships, and hookup behavior, and instead create families.

1.) Find ways daily to appreciate your yoni. During your menses, avoid complaining about your cramps, or saying that it sucks to be a woman or that you hate having a period. Be grateful that you are a part of the circle of life. Get in tune with your

137

actual cycle, not just the part where you shed your egg.

2.) Create criteria and have standards for whom you connect yourself with sexually. Make sure that he values you enough to create a family with you and call you his wife. Remember, "…women are the gate keepers of sex, which is one half of the mating equation…" (*Never Chase Men Again*, Bruce Bryans, pg.49)

Our yoni is one of our superpowers. Yes, our vaginas are powerful; relish the fact that you have one. Wars have been waged because of yoni power.

38. Surrender

*Love is an attempt at penetrating another
being, but it can only succeed if the surrender is
mutual.*
-Octavio Paz

Learning to surrender can be a difficult thing
to do, especially if you are used to calling your own
shots. Today's expert advice tells women to be
strong and relentless, to never give in. While these
tactics may work under certain circumstances, this
type of thinking absolutely will not work in a
relationship with a masculine man.

The man is the head and the woman is the
neck. Although the head is above the neck in
position, the head can't even turn without the neck.
There is power in the seemingly "lower" position;
the supporting role is often the most important role
of all. This is the beauty of yin/yang harmony.

When you are open to surrendering to your
man, you are open to his protection and provision.
This doesn't mean you have to be a doormat;
instead, it means that you understand the energy
flow and allow for it.

Surrender "…is not failure, defeat, holding up the white flag, or weakness, as it is traditionally defined. I define surrender as being able to give yourself wholly to something in a flow that's intuitively attuned. That means you make choices of what you want to flow with and what flow does not feel good…" (Judith Orloff, psychologytoday.com interview). "…a relationship with somebody that you want to love…when you decide I really want to go with this", "that's where surrender comes in, in terms of letting go more and more with your heart. Not being guarded, not keeping your foot on the brakes. Surrender means going with the flow of that relationship as best you can and not guarding your heart…"

Surrender is also something that must be practiced as a spiritual principle in order for blessings to flow. The art of surrendering is an important part of the universal laws of attraction. You must be willing to give up control and to trust the flow of spirit as it moves and brings you what you want and need. Refusal to surrender can keep your wheels spinning for years. Give up the need to be right and in control, to clear the path for magic to happen.

39. Forgive

Debate is masculine, conversation is feminine.
-         *Amos Bronson Alcott*

There is such a great deal of power in forgiveness. Like the spiritual principle of surrender, the spiritual principle of forgiveness can often be mistaken for weakness. However, granting forgiveness takes a great deal of personal fortitude and a heightened sense of spiritual consciousness.

In life, we will encounter people who are either unwilling or emotionally unable to love us. When we love another who is unwilling or unable to love us after we have loved them, it can hurt so badly. It can actually feel emotionally devastating.

The one thing I have learned after several failed relationships is that no one HAS to love you. There is no rule saying that just because you decide to love someone, they have to love you back. Their not loving you back isn't a crime, and it doesn't make them a bad person.

Forgive the men in your past who did not requite your love, understanding that the love you gave out will be returned another way, by another person. Unrequited love doesn't mean you are unlovable. Many times, when we find ourselves in relationships that don't feel good because we aren't being loved, they are signs from the universe that we must love ourselves more or grow in a particular area.

Viewing relationships as a learning place for how to love and how to receive love will help you open your heart to grant forgiveness. Not granting forgiveness keeps your heart closed. It keeps you bitter and angry, and prevents you from trusting men. And, quite frankly, this is not feminine; no man wants a bitter, angry woman.

As a beauty professional, I have worked with so many women over the years. There is nothing sadder than seeing a woman in her 50s who cannot experience joy and love because men hurt her in her 20s and she never forgave them.

Forgive Your Family

Let's be honest; some of the deepest emotional wounds come from people who are blood related to us. Sadly, we can't choose our family members, but we can choose to forgive them.

I'll be honest; growing up in my family, I didn't really feel loved, supported, or accepted. I was always an emotionally sensitive person, and I always liked living beyond African-American cultural limitations. I don't think I ever fit into my typical, southern-rooted, African-American family.

I also watched a lot of selfishness go on in my family between the haves and the have-nots: Family members who wouldn't let you borrow $1 to buy something off the dollar menu if you were truly in need, or who expected the $1 back with interest. I witnessed emasculation, gossiping, and unnecessary arguments between family memebers, as well as an overall lack of feminine nurturing and support, compounded by a spirit of negativity and a lack of trust in one another.

Although I knew if something serious were to happen, there were some family members I could depend on, I feel that I didn't receive the love, nurturing, or masculine protection a woman needs to be whole and emotionally healthy. Self-esteem is reinforced by those who raise you. I believe we are born with good self-esteem, but it is those we are surrounded by who tear that down or reinforce it.

I was abandoned by my father at a young age and didn't see him again until I was 13 years old. By that time, I hated him. I didn't see him or hear from him again for another four years after that, and again until I was around 23 or 24. My father not being there caused so many emotional issues and affected the type of men I attracted for a while, until I learned to forgive.

I remember the night I finally decided to confront my father about his abandoning me. I was living in Miami at the time, and I was sitting on my bed crying to my mother about feeling so empty inside because I didn't have a father. All my Latina friends had great, positive relationships and interactions with their dads. It seemed so normal. I had attended a friend's wedding that weekend (she was Latina), and it hit me that I didn't have a dad to walk me down the aisle if I ever got married, nor any man in my life who cared about me enough – or whom I cared for like a dad – to walk me down the aisle. It was such a heartbreaking moment.

My mom called my grandmother, who lived in Virginia, and told her to contact my dad because I was in the hospital and gravely ill. (I know that's messed up, but she had to think of a way to get him to call.) Within 15 minutes, my dad, whom I had not seen nor talked to since I was 17, called me and I started bawling. I finally had the chance to tell him how I felt after the years of neglect. It was scary, hard for me to say, and difficult for him to hear.

I was able to tell my father I did need him, and that I needed him more than every few years when he decided to call or show up at somebody's funeral. In the end, I opened my heart to forgive my dad because I realized he was a broken man who was struggling to make it, that his manly pride and the fact he felt so bad and ashamed about not being able to financially provide was one of the main factors that kept him away. I told him children appreciate time more than money if both cannot be given.

My dad and I have a good relationship now, almost 15 years later. He did walk me down the aisle at my wedding, and none of that would have been possible without forgiveness.

I've also been able to forgive my family in my heart by accepting there is a spirit of negativity in my family and there is not much I can do about it except love people at a distance, help people when absolutely necessary, show up at family functions when I can, and avoid participating in any drama or gossip. I realize most of my family members do not know who I am as a person, and that's fine. I have created my own family by adopting members who show real love and concern for me.

Forgive Yourself

You are perfectly imperfect. Give up on the idea that you have to "get it right," or that because you made so many mistakes you're a failure, or because you're not where you think you should be in your life by now you are failing at life.

Your journey is YOUR journey, and where you are is where you are supposed to be at the moment. You're not in a competition (feminine women don't compete with one another, remember), so stop stressing yourself out trying to keep up with the Joneses.

You must accept that: 1.) Life is an actual learning and growing process to teach you love and to elevate your soul, and 2.) You have the power inside you to have, do, or be whatever you want.

Be gentle with yourself. As the old saying goes, when you know better, you do better. The fact you are reading this book proves you are on the right path. Embrace every part of your glorious journey, including the mistakes.

40. Mind Your Manners

"Be fabulous."
— *__Lailah Gifty Akita__*

Having good manners is very important for the feminine woman. Good manners display a humbleness demonstrating you are considerate and you value other people. Good manners also show good upbringing, which is a direct reflection of the type family you grew up in.

Contrary to individualistic American thinking, you represent more than just yourself when you are out in public. You are also representing your husband (if married), his family, your family, and your children, and the same goes for them. If your behavior in public is less than pleasing, everyone is going to ask themselves, "Who raised her?"

I had a friend a few years back whose family was from India. She would never speak to strange men when she went out. She told me that in her community, all it took was one "auntie" (a term of endearment in their culture for an older woman) to see her doing something inappropriate or talking to someone she had no business talking to and it could ruin not only her chances of getting married into a good family, but her siblings' chances as well. She represented her family, and she took that seriously.

"Good manners are more than opening doors and writing thank you notes…Being polite and courteous means considering how others are feeling. If you practice good manners, you are showing those around you that you are considerate of their feelings and respectful. You are also setting standards for others' behavior and encouraging them to treat you with similar respect." (The Importance of Manners, www.mtstcil.org)

So, now that the why's of having good manners have been laid out, let's take a look at some basic manners applicable to our time in history and culture:

1.) When entering a room, make an effort to smile. Say hello and greet all the elders in the room first. Teach your children to do the same.

2.) Put away your cell phones when talking to someone or at dinner. Learn the art of conversation. One thing that blew my mind when I traveled in France was that people sat for HOURS at cafes and restaurants, and nobody was on their phones. It was a stark contrast to our smartphone-obsessed country.

3.) Say "please" and "thank you." Extremely basic, but it's something people forget from time to time. Also be sure to say "please" and "thank you" when texting and sending emails.

4.) Keep personal conversations and arguments off social media. It's petty and childish. This is what private messaging, texting, emails, and face-to-face conversation are for.

5.) If you need to discipline your child, do so in private. Public beat downs in our culture are talked about with pride, but I personally feel that public humiliation is a residual effect of slavery.

6.) RSVP to the parties and events to which you are invited. The host(ess) is counting on that information to properly plan the event

7.) Tip at least 15%. If you don't have enough to tip, don't go. It's extremely rude to not tip. If you are bad at math, download a tip app.

8.) Dress appropriately for the occasion. As a rule of thumb, it is better to be overdressed than underdressed.

9.) Learn formal place settings for the table. You should know the difference between a salad fork and a dinner fork, and what to do with your napkin upon sitting down at a table.

10.)Do bring a hostess gift when invited over to someone's house for dinner or otherwise. A bottle of wine, flowers, or chocolates are excellent choices.

11.)Do not do your makeup in public or at the dinner table. Excuse yourself to the restroom or powder room to freshen up. Touching up lip gloss or lightly touching up your lipstick are the only exceptions

12.)Wait until everyone has been seated AND served food before you start eating. The only exception is if it's a very long table; in this case, you may start eating after five to seven people are seated and served.

13.)If you don't drink alcohol or wine, simply place your wine glass upside down. This is the universal code for "I won't be drinking tonight."

14.)Eat a little bit of whatever is offered to you, even if it looks a bit weird. Can you imagine First Lady Michelle Obama or an African queen representing her country sitting down at an elegant dinner in an exotic country and saying, "Ugh, that looks nasty, I ain't eating that"? Um, no, you can't, so take a small taste, swallow quickly, and wash it down discreetly.

15.)Take the time to learn the cultural mannerisms of any country to which you may be traveling. The world does not revolve around the United States of America. Often this type of snobbery gives Americans a bad name.

16.)Serve all the men their food first, starting with the eldest male, then your man (if you have one). This will get you A LOT of points with the men in the room. Be prepared for backlash from some of the women, but a feminine woman should honor this tradition.

41. Femininity in the Workplace

Women should not have to adopt masculine traits in order to succeed. You should be able to stay as a woman, and in tune with your femininity, and still be equal. - Isla Fisher

Modern feminist thinking has women wanting to be "Boss Chicks" and hustlers who grind with no sleep. Hook, line, and sinker, many women are buying into the idea that, in order to succeed, they must take on masculine qualities.

A woman CAN succeed in the business arena while leading with her feminine energy. You can also use your feminine energy to connect with males in your work environment, including male students, if you are an educator.

Here are a few tips to utilize. Feel the power of your femininity at work:

1.) When working with men, talk less. Men are visual, and your message can be better conveyed visually. Also, in meetings, talking less shows humility and that you are not self-absorbed.
2.) In meetings, serve the men something, be it coffee, tea, mints, or snacks, and make it obvious (without

being TOO obvious) that you are serving. This will give you an extreme amount of power – feminine power.

3.) Smile+Touch+Eye Contact = Positive Attention and Co-Operation. It shows you are warm, nurturing, and resilient, and it gets you the deal.

4.) When you talk, do so in a low, feminine voice and choose your words deliberately and wisely.

5.) When greeting men, shake firmly and place your other hand on top or practice a two-handed handshake. (Diagram/Picture)

6.) Dress in a feminine way, but do NOT show skin (e.g., cleavage, too much leg/thigh). Your reasons for doing so may be misinterpreted.

7.) Do wear soft, movable hair that is clean and that smells good.

8.) Wear earrings,

9.) Wear lip gloss and light makeup, and look polished.

10.)Have good business manners and table etiquette for business dinners.

11.)Use titles when addressing people in the room.

12.)Don't dumb yourself down; the goal is to be warm, feminine, AND intelligent.

42. Queen Mother

Femininity in and of itself - and the feminine - can be not only privileged, but honored or worshipped. - Jill Soloway

Our children are the jewels in our crowns, our babies. We want the best for them, and to see them grow up and be great.

As Queen Mother in your house, it is key to remember you are raising someone else's spouse and parent, and the way you treat your children will affect many people for several generations after you are gone from the physical realm.

Generational excellence should be the goal when parenting, if you come from a family with a lot of generational bondage, you must make an extra effort to gather new information and add new tools to your treasure chest to create a new path for your children, grandchildren, and beyond.

Emasculating Your Son

This is one topic that breaks my heart. When I think of mothers emasculating their sons, I picture a video clip that was widely broadcast on the news of an African-American woman beating her son in public, after he participated in some neighborhood riots. Lots of people, including news anchors, praised her behavior. Lots of African-American people praised her behavior. I did not.

My first question was, where was this boy's father? The second thought that came to mind was that this mother had basically destroyed her son's manhood publically, and may have humiliated him for the rest of his life. Here we had a teenaged boy who was in the midst of discovering and defining his manhood, and his mother beat him on national TV. She may have made him unfit to even be someone's husband, all in 15 minutes.

I see black women all the time bragging about how they slap, beat, and cuss out their children. I ask how this is normal? How is this feminine-style parenting or effective parenting?

You cannot expect your children to have king and queen mentality if you treat them like peasants. If we are the African Queens we love to say we are, we need to abolish slave-mentality parenting. Our ancestors were beaten and cussed out, and this (in my opinion) has created a legacy of beatings and negative words spewed out at our precious seeds. And honestly, if beatings worked so well, we would have the best-behaved, best-mannered people on planet earth…but we don't.

Take parenting classes. If we are willing to attend school to be a nurse, or take continuing education classes for advanced degrees to get ahead at work, why not take classes to enhance our skills as parents?

Learn effective frustration management skills; that way you won't feel the need to automatically cuss out your children. Stay feminine and allow your husband to discipline the kids when he is at home. Have a team parenting style in which the children know you are both on the same page with respect to the house rules, and that when your husband is not present, they are to respect you and treat you delicately.

If you are a single mother, reach out for help, and enlist the help of good, honorable men in your family, church or community to help out with your children from time to time. I also advise single mothers, that if you have a good relationship with your child/ren's father, that you have your sons especially, to live primarily with their father after the age of 10. It is at this age that boys start really looking for examples of manhood and NEED to be around other emotionally healthy men. Boys learn how to be men from watching other men. A boy raised in a house full of women may have a confused sense of masculinity, and this may render him unfit to be another woman's husband.

We must also discuss being more selective about whom we have children with in the first place, placing a high priority on getting married and THEN having children with men who can actually provide for and protect the family unit. Even single moms should make an effort to become part of a nuclear family and throw away these ideas that it's best to wait until your children are grown to get involved with a man or that you don't need a man. Statistics show that children who grow up with a father in the home, or a good stepfather, have higher self-esteem and marital success rates.

We must also make an effort to protect the femininity of our daughters. Allow them to be soft and delicate, and educate them in every way possible so they are intelligent and resilient. Stop telling them to toughen up. Sadly, we are grooming our girls to live without a man, a husband, a protector. This must end. Girls should grow up knowing that they are worthy of being protected and expecting men to protect them.

By the age of 18, our daughters should know what to look for in a husband, understand what it takes to be a good wife and mother, and understand that the role of Queen Mother is just as, if not more important that seeking advanced degrees. We simply cannot afford to keep raising generations of women who glorify boyfriends, and think their bachelor's degree is enough to wing an entire marriage.

These are crucial times we are in, and the role of the Queen Mother has never been more important. If we are to make any sort of real cultural recovery, we must use our femininity to nurture our seeds into becoming the best they can possibly be.

Final Thoughts

It is more important than ever that, as black women, we embrace the power of our feminine essence. Our health, our wealth, our love lives, the generational excellence of our families, and the detriment of our community all depend on how well we can utilize our feminine essence to nurture those around us and bridge the great divide with other communities.

As women, we are so very important. There is a wonderful Islamic proverb that I love, it says; The man is the head, but the woman is the neck. Meaning that the man leads, but cannot turn or navigate properly without the woman.

I hope *The Black Girl's Guide to being Blissfully Feminine* helps you put away the notion you need to be strong, take on everyone's problems, and work yourself to death. I hope you are inspired to be girly, laugh, play, and enjoy life as a woman. I hope you see the beauty in being a feminine woman, and are empowered to create a life of beauty and magic – Black Girl Magic, that is.

About The Author

Candice is a femininity educator, certified life coach, and beauty professional from Cleveland, Ohio. Currently residing in sunny Florida, Candice has studied femininity and masculinity for over 10 years. It has become a passion of hers to help women tap into the power of their feminine essence to attract deeper, more intimate relationships with men, foster genuine sisterhood with other women, and have more overall confidence as a woman.

Candice absolutely loves teaching women to enjoy being feminine women. She is a traditional woman, with traditional family values, and her overall goal in life is to add value to the lives of others, and make them feel beautiful. She hopes to meet you at a Modern Day Geisha workshop very soon!

Blissfully Feminine Workshops

You can go to <u>www.blissfullyfeminine.com</u> to join the Domestic Goddess Society or enroll in a Modern Day Geisha Workshop near you!

Modern Day Geisha workshops are designed to help you tap into your juicy feminine essence so you can attract the right man, improve your existing marriage, be magnetic, and foster genuine sisterhood with other women. Hope to see you at a workshop very soon!

54377373R00090

Made in the USA
Lexington, KY
12 August 2016